FLOODED WITH LIGHT

A STUDY OF EPHESIANS

GINA GREEN

ISBN 978-1-7325-2860-4

Cover Design: Chris Angrisani
Interior Design: Gina Green

Acknowledgements

There would be no Ephesians study if not for several friends who have encouraged me throughout the years to keep pursuing revelation of the King and His Kingdom.

Christy, Rachel and Kaf - you three were with me at the beginning of it all. God seemed to awaken all of us and we just grabbed each others' hands and started to run together. The three of you hold a special place in my heart as you refused to let me back off when I was afraid or facing opposition or slowly being mesmerized by life. Your friendship and encouragement are part of my foundation; you helped to establish a vision within me for the destiny God had laid before me. Thank you for your friendship and God-love!

Kim, that afternoon in the bookstore in the Fall of 2014 was a *kairos* moment in my life. Your words, as I remember them: "If you can't find the type of study you are looking for, then you know what you have to do." Oh, that feeling in my gut! A slow, quiet whisper emerged, "I have to write it." Thank you for your friendship, encouragement, and positive Kingdom perspective.

Marci, thank you for that telephone call in January, 2015. Your invitation to study together was the catalyst for actual words to be put to paper.

Karen and Ruthann, thank you for inviting me into leadership of our women's Bible study and then trusting me to facilitate this Ephesians study. You helped me step over my utter terror of failing and continually encouraged me to keep writing. Thank you for believing in me.

Yun, thank you for your courage in sharing with me the true impact this study had on your spiritual life. Of course it made me feel good that people liked the material or liked the format or liked the weekly group discussion, but more than anything else, I was looking for transformational effect. I did not want to impart information only—there are people writing Bible studies that are more academically qualified to do that. **I wanted to share personal revelation that acted as a doorway into a lifestyle of revelation**. I needed at least one person to walk through that doorway. You were the one.

Adam, I was surprised when you asked me for a copy of the study to work through. I was not prepared for such overwhelming support. Often I found myself a little shell-shocked at your dedication to the material - working every question, recording every personal encounter (in detail *and* with illustrations), highlighting favorite sections, etc. You gave it the same level of attention you would give to a "real" study—like a John Paul Jackson course! Words could not have encouraged me or made me feel loved more than those actions. Thank you for always being for me, always finding ways to support who I am and causing me to prosper. I'm glad we're on this Kingdom adventure together.

A very special thanks to the women's Bible study group at NewSong church. You were the first group to work through this material—your graciousness towards me was extraordinary.

Contents

Introduction

A note about your approach to Scripture...

2 Timothy 3:16 tells us that all Scripture is given by inspiration of God and profitable for doctrine, reproof, correction and training in righteousness. There is a way to understand that particular verse that leaves one a little cold, as if the Scriptures are only instructions to be read and obeyed, regardless of understanding. However, there is a depth to the phrase "training in righteousness" that goes beyond traditional obedience and brings a greater level of Life. Since the beginning of my journey into the Kingdom of God, I have been fascinated with "the ways"—the ways of God, the ways of the Kingdom, the ways of righteousness, the ways in which Jesus did things when He walked the earth, the ways in which the Kingdom manifests itself in our midst now. My personal understanding of the concept of "becoming like Jesus" has everything to do with coming into alignment with His ways.

Alignment with the ways of God is not about following a checklist. It is about being tuned to His heart. His heart is synonymous with His ways, for they are inextricably linked. What He does is the fruit of Who He is; searching out His ways is one way we can be, like King David, "after His heart." Our training under the tutelage of the knowledge of good and evil taught us to look toward what we had to *do* in life, but in the New Covenant, the Holy Spirit teaches us something altogether different. **The Holy Spirit teaches us *who to be.***

The ways of God are about whom to be. One aspect of being trained in righteousness is being renewed in your mind so that your mind is in agreement with your spirit in the ways of God, thereby bringing transformation into your life. In light of that, I encourage you to read Ephesians with your heart open to discovering more of His ways. Purposefully yield yourself to the influential light of the Holy Spirit.

In His light we see light.

Psalm 36:9

Eyes Wide Open

Week One

- ♦A Bird's-Eye View
- ♦New Identity
- ♦Spirit of Wisdom & Understanding
- ♦Eyes Flooded with Light
- ♦To Know

Day 1

A Bird's-Eye View

As we begin to study Paul's letter to the Ephesians, I want to emphasize that it is a letter. Would you read a newly received personal letter just a few paragraphs at a time? Even if you revisited parts of that letter for a specific reason, would you not do so with the full context of the letter in mind?

If you have been studying the Bible for any amount of time, you have probably studied much of it topically. Typically, studying topically is piecing together what Scripture teaches on any given topic by collecting appropriate verses from throughout the Bible to get a complete picture regarding that topic. It is a valid and valuable form of study. I caution against it being your primary or only form of study. When studying the Bible, context is everything. Even memorizing individual Scriptures can be less than beneficial if the meaning is not understood first within context.

In an effort to see the whole before we examine the parts, please read through all six chapters of Ephesians in one sitting. Be purposeful about gaining a bird's-eye perspective. For those of you who have been studying the Bible for a while, this next request will be hard if not nearly impossible: Try to disregard chapter subheadings and any commentary your Bible may provide.

When studying the Bible, context is everything.

What is Paul's purpose for writing the letter?

What are some concepts within the letter that catch your attention?

Without paying attention to chapter headings and subheadings, did you notice something new or gain a new perspective on previously familiar sections of Scripture?

Day 2

New Identity

For the rest of this week we will focus on Ephesians chapter one, although I recommend reading the entire letter every few days to keep the full context in mind. I realize that it is time-consuming and can be difficult to remain attentive through all six chapters. Some of the difficulty is in Paul's lengthy sentences, and some is in the fact that we are not used to reading the whole thing through! You can do it.

Although the letter is written specifically to the church in Ephesus, everything Paul states relating to them being believers also applies to us as believers. This chapter is full of identity gems.

As you read each statement below, paraphrase in your own words what the statement means to you in this season of your life. In verses 3-8 we discover that as believers we are:

Blessed with all spiritual blessings in the heavenlies in Christ

Chosen in Him before the foundation of the world so that we should be holy & blameless before Him in love

Predestined to adoption according to God's good pleasure

Accepted in the beloved

Redeemed through Jesus' blood

Forgiven of sins

Lavished upon with grace that abounds towards us

You could spend a day meditating on any one of these concepts before moving on. Seriously. Each of the previous statements can become life-changing realities with some focus and intentionality.

There is plenty more to glean from verses 9-14.

> *"[9]He made known to us the mystery of His will, according to His kind intention which He purposed in Him [10]with a view to an administration suitable to the fullness of times, that is, the summing up of all things on the earth. In Him [11]also we have obtained an inheritance, having been predestined according to His purpose who works all things after the counsel of His will, [12]to the end that we who were the first to hope in Christ would be to the praise of His glory. [13]In Him, you also, after listening to the message of truth, the gospel of your salvation - having also believed, you were sealed in Him with the Holy Spirit of promise, [14]who is given as a pledge of our inheritance, with a view to redemption of God's own possession, to the praise of His glory."*

Take some time to select some verses within this section, write them out, meditate on them and make them into declarations over yourself. Some identity statements will mean more to you than others in this season of your life. Focus on those! Ask the Holy Spirit for grace to believe that you are who He says you are *on a whole new level.*

Revelation is ever increasing. Declaring truth over yourself is like kneading yeast into dough. You are kneading truth into your thinking, your believing, your perceiving. As you do this, the truth permeates your being and becomes established as part of your foundation.

Day 3

Spirit of Wisdom & Understanding

"The Spirit of the LORD will rest on Him, the spirit of wisdom and understanding, the spirit of counsel and strength, the spirit of knowledge and the fear of the LORD."

Isaiah 11:2

Again, read chapter one. In verse 15 we discover that the church in Ephesus is known for their faith in Jesus and love toward each other—their God-type-of-love (agape). And Paul is thankful that they are prospering; yet there is always more. We are always being propelled forward in the Kingdom. Paul launches into what we now refer to as one of his apostolic prayers:

> *"...[17]that the God of our Lord Jesus Christ, the Father of glory, may give to you the spirit of wisdom and revelation in the knowledge of Him. [18]That the eyes of your understanding would be enlightened, so that you will know what is the hope of His calling, the riches of the glory of His inheritance in the saints [19]and what is the surpassing greatness of His power toward us who believe. In accordance with the working of the strength of His might [20]which He brought about in Christ, when He raised Jesus from the dead and seated Him at His right hand in the heavenly places..."*

Breaking down these verses gives additional insight into the dramatic request Paul has just made on behalf of the Ephesian believers. He has asked God to give the Ephesians five specific things:

1. A spirit of wisdom & revelation in the knowledge of Him **so that**
2. The eyes of their understanding would be enlightened
3. They would know the hope of His calling
4. They would know the riches of the glory of His inheritance in the saints
5. They would know the exceeding greatness of His power toward believers

Let's take a look at each one of these separately, starting with verse 17.

> *"...[17]that the God of our Lord Jesus Christ, the Father of glory, may give to you the spirit of wisdom and revelation in the knowledge of Him.*

In your own words, what is the difference between wisdom and revelation?

Since Paul is writing to a group of believers, especially believers who are known for their **faith in Jesus** (1:15), he is obviously not referring to the "knowledge of Him" in terms of initial salvation knowledge. He is asking the Holy Spirit to give an even bigger revelatory understanding of God: His ways, His purposes, and His love. This request is one that we can forever make, on behalf of others and for ourselves.

For every revelation we receive about God, there is yet another. For every encounter we have with His love, there is another. **Our understanding of who He is will be ever increasing**. (Isaiah 9:6-7; Matthew 13:31-33) Ever increasing is a way of the Kingdom.

Here are some concepts for you to meditate on today:

Who is Jesus to you during this season of your life? What aspect of Him is being emphasized to you by the Holy Spirit? What aspect of Him do you desire to come into alignment with? Specifically ask the Holy Spirit to increase your experiential knowledge of Jesus in *that* area. Record your thoughts.

"For a child will be born to us, a son will be given to us. And the government will rest on His shoulders. His name will be called Wonderful Counselor, Mighty God, Eternal Father, Prince of Peace. There will be no end to the increase of His government or of peace."

Isaiah 9:6-7

As we go through seasons of life we are always increasing in the knowledge of Jesus—continually seeing Him in a deeper way.

If that exercise was difficult or unfruitful then the next exercise should help.

Something to consider...

The following exercise will help you access grace in order to receive from God. Set aside some time to:

"And when He had said this, He breathed on them and said to them, "Receive the Holy Spirit. If you forgive the sins of any, their sins have been forgiven them; if you retain the sins of any, they have been retained."

John 20:22-23

Ask God if there is a **lie** you believe about Him in the area of revelation you are seeking. If something comes to mind then:

- Ask **where/how you learned to believe** that lie. Often, the lie is not something you are consciously walking around believing. It has been hidden, sometimes by pain, sometimes by time. Perhaps a memory will come to mind. If so:

  ◊ **Forgive** where forgiveness is needed. Forgive any persons involved. Forgive yourself for believing the lie. You may need to forgive God for a perception that He allowed the situation/occurrence, etc. Freely forgive as the Holy Spirit brings it to your attention.

  ◊ Then **renounce** that lie and verbally **come out of agreement** with it.

  ◊ Ask the Holy Spirit to reveal the **truth**. Remember, any truth that the Holy Spirit reveals will be in alignment with who Jesus is and with Father God as Jesus revealed Him to be. Intentionally receive grace from God to **believe** this truth.

- Ask Jesus to **heal** any wounds that may have occurred and **redeem** any effects that believing the lie brought about in your life and the lives of others.

I recommend purposefully soaking and **meditating on the truth** that the Holy Spirit revealed. That truth is an aspect of Jesus because He is the Truth (John 14:6). Knead that truth into your soul. The experiential knowledge of Jesus brings transformation. You are destined to be transformed (Romans 8:29). This exercise is an example of partnering with the Holy Spirit in your transformation process.

Day 4

Eyes Flooded with Light

Read Ephesians chapter one again today. Remember that even as you are reading you are kneading truth into your soul and spirit.

Let's continue to break down Paul's prayer in verses 17-23 specifically focusing on the first part of verse 18:

> *"[18]That the **eyes** of your **understanding** would be **enlightened**..."*

Eyes. The Spirit has some interesting things to say about eyes in the New Testament. Time for a quick topical study.

- *"If your right **eye** makes you stumble (brings offense), tear it out and throw it from you..." -Matthew 5:29*
- *"The **eye** is the lamp of the body so then if your eye is clear your whole body will be full of light..." -Matthew 6:22*
- *"But if your **eye** is bad your whole body will be full of darkness..." -Matthew 6:23*
- *"Why do you look at the speck that is in your brother's **eye**, but do not notice the log that is in your own eye?" -Matthew 7:3*

In all of the verses cited above the original Greek word translated "eye" is *ophthalmos* (G3788). Strong's Greek Dictionary defines it as the following:

> Ophthalmos—the eye (figurative or literal); by implication *vision*; figuratively *envy* (from the jealous side glance);—eye, sight.

It can mean your literal eyeball and it can also mean your vision. Either way, it is **the way in which you see**. In Matt 13:14 and Mark 4:12 Jesus relates our hearing to understanding and our seeing to perceiving. So, at the very least, in the four Scriptures above, Jesus is emphasizing that the way in which we see or perceive **is important**.

- If the way in which you see causes you to be offended (or causes others to be offended) then get rid of it. A perspective that is filled with offense will not lead to Life.
- The way in which you see will either bring light or darkness into your body, your life, and your circumstances.

- The way in which you see can get clogged up, so walk in humility and check for clogs before trying to unclog someone else's vision. Often, our own clog so distorts our vision that we see clogs everywhere we look. That's a sure sign that the problem may be ours.

As our minds are renewed and we see according to the Spirit of Truth, as with a clear eye (Matt 6:22), we will increasingly be in alignment with God and His Kingdom.

"The eye is the lamp of the body. So then if your eye is clear, your whole body will be full of light."

Matthew 6:22

Now Paul specifically prays that the eyes of their *understanding* would be enlightened—the original Greek word that has been translated as understanding/mind/heart (depending on the translation) is *dianoia* (G1271). It is used 13 times in the New Testament. Strong's Greek dictionary defines it as follows:

> Dianoia—deep thought, properly the faculty[1] (mind or its disposition); by implication its exercise:—imagination, mind, understanding.

There are several words in the New Testament that are often translated as understanding but they do not all mean the same thing. Let's take a look at *dianoia.*

Write out the Scriptures referenced below to get a feel for how the word is used.

Matthew 22:37

Luke 10:27

Ephesians 4:18

Colossians 1:21

Hebrews 8:10

2 Peter 3:11

1 John 5:20

[1] Faculty - an ability for a particular kind of action; an inherent capability of the body

There are some interesting lessons learned after studying this word. In the New American Standard Bible (NASB), *dianoia* is most often translated as "mind," although I would suggest you think of it as "mindset" or ways of thinking (which directly relate to our ways of believing).

- Along with our heart, our soul and our strength we are to love God with all of our *dianoia*. Notice it is **distinct from** the heart and the soul. I wish I could frame this particular point in a neon flashing light! We are to love God with the way our minds see. **A Kingdom mindset is not optional.**
- Our *dianoia* is darkened when we are alienated from the Life of God or *in any area* that is separated from the Life of God.
- In addition to our hearts, the *dianoia* is where God has promised to write His laws.
- The *dianoia* can be pure. The word translated as "pure" in 2 Peter 3:1 actually means *"judged by sunlight"*.

So, what's the point? **There is a way in which our minds see or perceive.** Our perception ultimately affects our understanding. If you have received the gift of righteousness, then you have a new heart—your mind is being renewed, renovated, and restructured. The way in which your mind sees and perceives is changing. A new understanding is the result. You have been **made new** (2 Corinthians 5:17) and are in the process of learning how to **think new**, which will cause you to act like the new creation that you are. You might say this is one way that we "work out your salvation" (Philippians 2:12).

A Kingdom mindset is not optional.

In the parable of the Sower, as written in Matthew, the good soil that enables the seed to flourish and produce fruit is interpreted by Jesus Himself to be *understanding—that which your thinking/believing stands upon*. The point of a renewed mind is that you gain right understanding of the King, His Kingdom and His ways, and that His ways become your ways. Yes, His ways are "higher than our ways" when "our ways" are not Kingdom ways, but ***it is not to remain that way***! **His ways are becoming your ways as you become more and more like Him.** Every aspect of a renewed mind bears Kingdom fruit and releases His glory. And by the phrase "releases His glory," I mean reveals who He is to the world around us.

Our minds have eyes, perspectives, lenses. Paul is asking that they be enlightened. The Amplified Bible translates enlightened as "flooded with light." I love that image! The point of flooding the ways we think with light is that we would rightly see or rightly perceive. When we see rightly, or *righteously*, we see clearly and without corruption.

"I pray that the eyes of your understanding may be enlightened..."

Ephesians 1:18 (KJV)

Can you look back over the past 5 years and identify any area in your thinking in which your perspective changed regarding spiritual things? Think of Scriptures that you understand differently now than perhaps even a year ago. The words in the Scripture did not change, but your understanding of those words changed. Perhaps it was a Kingdom concept that came alive in your life and suddenly you "got it" and now can see it in the life of Jesus and the disciples as never before. It was as if the written Word of God took on flesh and walked around in your life. Now you, your perspective, and your understanding have changed and you see life differently.

On this page and the next, take some time to identify some of these markers in your life. Those lens corrections, if you will, are testimonies of what God has done in your life. They are just as significant as physical healings, marriage miracles, and every other supernatural thing. They are part of your story, your personal transformation. Remember and be glad (Psalm 119:2)!

Day 5

To Know

Again, read through Ephesians chapter one with purpose, with a single eye (focused).

Continuing with verse 18:

> *"[18]...that you would know what is* ***the hope of His calling****, what are* ***the riches of the glory of His inheritance in the saints*** *[19]and what is* ***the exceeding greatness of His power toward us*** *who believe..."*

There are three specific things that Paul is asking for in this part of his prayer, three things that he would like the Ephesian believers, as well as you and me, to know and ***understand rightly*** (eyes flooded with light): 1) **purpose** (His calling for you), 2) **identity** (His inheritance within you), and 3) **power** (His action toward you). I humbly submit that these three things are central to a Kingdom foundation of thinking, believing, and living. How you understand your purpose, your identity and the power of God will determine what you do and don't do here on the earth regarding the Kingdom of God.

What do you think Paul means by "the hope of His calling"? Is he simply praying that you would rightly understand your calling from God, or is he going for something more significant? How could God's calling on your life bring hope, either to you or to others? Has it already done so?

Again, why "the glory of His inheritance" rather than "His inheritance"? Is there a difference, and if so, what is that difference?

Have you ever thought about how God's power operates? Does He delegate some for you to use at will, or is it all controlled from the throne room of heaven? Does He release His power as you release your faith? Is He making a decision each time you pray to release power or not? What kinds of things would He consider if that was the economy of God? Why do you believe what you believe in this area?

Thoughts?

Purpose

Purpose is multidimensional in the Kingdom of God. We can find several purposes for mankind throughout Scripture: relationship with God, relationship with one another, destroying the works of the devil (including healing the sick, raising the dead, casting out demons), and glorifying God, to name a few. As a whole, mankind is to have dominion over all the earth, and be instrumental in releasing the government of the Kingdom until all the kingdoms of the world have become subject to the Kingdom of God.

"Heal the sick, raise the dead, cleanse the lepers, cast out demons. Freely you received, freely give."

Matthew 10:8

What is your particular role in that? What piece are you within the whole? What's your *personal* calling?

Have you ever had an encounter where you perceived that God was "calling" you or revealing to you your purpose on the earth? How is that different from perceiving an assignment from God, if at all?

Identity

Doesn't it always come back to identity? Who we think we are versus who we actually are is a primary place of contention within us. Sometimes, in an authentic attempt at humility, we try to not think of ourselves as having any worth. We don't want to "think more of ourselves than we ought," so we try to balance the scales by remembering all the ways in which we don't measure up. But Jesus paid a high price for us because we **do** have worth! And paying that price bought Him something—it bought Him the right to give us the gift of His own righteousness. When we receive that gift, we receive quite an inheritance—His inheritance. It's a two-way gift: He gains us as part of His inheritance and we gain Him as our inheritance. We need right understanding of both!

The key to humility in all of this is remembering where the righteousness and inheritance come from—they are gifts from Jesus Himself. They don't come forth from you but are given **to** you *for a purpose*. Who you are in light of His righteousness is your truest identity.

Can you identify several ways in recent years that He has revealed your identity to you? Dreams in the night? Experiences in His Presence that impart an increase of knowledge to you? Specific passages of Scripture that He has highlighted to you and emphasized in your life?

Who you are in light of His righteousness is your truest identity.

What was the fruit of those encounters? Has learning aspects of whom you really are caused you to think differently or behave differently? Record some specific examples.

Remembering specific examples will bring encouragement and should also provide some sort of measurement for you. True change within us will eventually produce observable change to those around us.

Power

The power of God is a fascinating subject. We don't have to understand how it works in order to experience it in our lives, but I suspect that understanding certain aspects of the power of God might increase our consistency in releasing it into others' lives. Understanding the power of God must be significant or Paul wouldn't have requested that the Ephesians' understanding of it be flooded with light.

Have you had experiences with the power of God? If so, briefly record some of them.

Finally, consider verse 22:

"[22]And He put all things in subjection under His feet..."

Take a look at 1 Corinthians 15:25 and Hebrews 2:8. What does this reveal to us about this subjection?

Established

Week Two

♦You've Come A Long Way

♦The Obedience of Faith

♦A Gift of God

♦Good Works

♦The Foundation

Day 1

You've Come A Long Way

This week the focus will be on chapter two, but please read through the entire letter in one sitting before zeroing in on chapter two. Remember, chapter two is part of a whole, and needs to be kept in context.

For the rest of Ephesians, Paul is expanding on the very things He has asked God to release by revelation to the Ephesians: identity, purpose and power. Try to keep these things in mind as you purposefully read through the remaining chapters.

The bird's-eye view of chapter two: We've come a long way! Verse 1 starts us off with being dead, verses 19-22 leave us as part of God's household. Redemption is truly abundant.

Identity, Purpose, and Power

Let's begin with 2:1. No beating around the bush here. Before all the good stuff Paul wrote about in chapter one happened **to** you and **within** you, "*you were dead in trespasses and sins…*"

> Trespasses = G3900 paraptoma—*a side slip* (lapse or deviation), that is (unintentional) *error* or (willful) *transgression.*
>
> Sins = G266 hamartia—*sin* (properly abstract); offense, sin(-ful).

This includes the things you didn't know about, the things you did know about and everything in between. No one escaped.

Continuing with verse 2,

> "[2]*in which you formerly walked according to the course of this world, according to the prince of the power of the air, of the spirit that is now working in the sons of disobedience.*"
>
> > Prince = G758 archon—a first (in rank or power); chief (ruler), magistrate, prince, ruler.
> >
> > power = G1849 exousia—authority, jurisdiction.

There are at least five root words in the New Testament that are translated "power." Those five words are:

1. *exousia*—delegated authority (used 93 times)
2. *dunamis*—miraculous dynamite power (used 116 times)

3. *energia*—energy (used 8 times)
4. *kratos*—dominion (used 12 times)
5. *ischus*—strength (used 11 times)

Though it is not wrong to translate them as "power," for each are most definitely a form of power, the words *do* have different nuances that affect our understanding. Included below is a list of some of the references for each word in the NT. I personally find it helpful to mark in my Bible the specific Greek word used when translated as *power*. For a complete list, see appendix A.

I suggest you go through at least five Scripture references for each of the five words (see below) to get a feel for their differences.

Exousia (G1849): Matt 7:29; John 19:10; John 19:11; Acts 5:4; Acts 8:19; Acts 26:18; Rom 9:21; Rev 11:6;

Dunamis (G1411): Matt 6:13; Matt 25:15; Mark 6:5; Acts 1:8; 1Cor 12:28; 1Cor14:11; 2Cor 1:8; 2Cor 12:9;

Energia (G1753): Eph 1:19; Eph 3:7; Eph 4:16; Php 3:21; Col 1:29; Col 2:12; 2Th 2:9; 2Th 2:11;

Kratos (G2904): Luk 1:51; Acts 19:20; Eph 1:19; Eph 6:10; Col 1:11; 1Tim 6:16; Heb 2:14; 1Pe 4:11; 1Pe 5:11; Jud 1:25; Rev 1:6; Rev 5:13;

Ischus (G2479): Mar 12:30; Mar 12:33; Luk 10:27; Eph 1:19; Eph 6:10; 2Th 1:9; 1Pe 4:11; 2Pe 2:11; Rev 5:12; Rev 7:12; Rev 18:2;

Were there any surprises as you discovered the *type* of power described in the Scriptures you researched? Were there any instances in this exercise where your understanding of a Scripture changed?

Returning to Ephesians 2:2, Paul is making the point that there is a "prince of the …air" that has *authority* to rule in that place. Before you became a believer you were under the influence of the authority that ruled in whatever atmosphere you found yourself. But you have been changed and now have the opportunity to live from a different atmosphere—one where you have been "blessed with every spiritual blessing" (Eph 1:3) and with the One who is "above all rule and authority (*exousia*) and power (*dunamis*)…" (Eph 1:21).

There are two aspects I would like to highlight regarding the atmosphere in which we find ourselves.

- The first is the spiritual atmosphere in the physical places in which we move around. Our homes have an atmosphere, our schools have atmospheres, and our shopping malls have atmospheres. Every existing place has an atmosphere. There's a particular bulk warehouse that has a very distinct atmosphere. Every time I enter this store I am aware of the strength of the influence this atmosphere has on me. It's one of urgency. The lanes are full and the super sized carts are moving fast. I don't have to "choose" to partner with this atmosphere—it apprehends me. However, because I belong to another Kingdom, I have the opportunity to choose **not** to partner with it **once I become aware of it**. Instead, I can access a supernatural peace because of my connection to the Holy Spirit, and not only enjoy peace during my time in that store, but also release peace to anyone near me because I am a radiator of the Kingdom within me. When I am successful at transitioning from the atmosphere that everyone else is experiencing to the atmosphere provided by the Kingdom of God, then I have just *shifted my atmosphere,* demonstrating that the "prince of the …air" is not the prince of *my* air.

- The second aspect of atmosphere is our access into the heavenly realms. This is more than just our connection to the Holy Spirit; we can actually step into another dimension by faith. Sometimes we step into another dimension, sometimes something from that dimension steps into our dimension and faith enables us to see it.

"…The kingdom of the world has become the Kingdom of our Lord and of His Christ…"

Revelation 11:15

Have you experienced either aspects of shifting atmospheres? Is the idea of choosing your atmosphere new to you? If so, can you think of times where it would have been nice to be able to access an atmosphere of peace or joy rather than experience the atmosphere that was manifesting around you?

Have you experienced any aspect of living *from* the atmosphere of heaven? What does that mean to you?

Now, are there aspects of living from the atmosphere of heaven that you have *not* experienced but have heard of or read about through the testimony of others or the Scriptures and *would like to* experience?

Personal testimony

One evening, while we were hosting a small group meeting in our home, my husband encouraged everyone to close his or her eyes and soak in the Presence of God. I closed my eyes and found myself imagining an angel in the room. I didn't set out to imagine an angel. In fact, I thought my mind had wandered and rather than "reel it back in" I did something unusual for me—I just let it play out. The angel was so tall that I couldn't see his head. Somehow I knew he had blonde hair, even though I couldn't see it. Also, he had a yellow sash that ran diagonally across his torso that read "Justice." When the designated soaking time ended my husband asked for testimonies of what anyone had experienced. I did not speak up because I assumed that it was just my imagination. At the end of our meeting we did a prophetic exercise in which you have a very short amount of time to interact with the Holy Spirit and release an encouraging word for your partner. That night we did that exercise repeatedly until everyone had both received a word and given a word to every other person in the group. Imagine my surprise when one of my partners told me that he was hearing only one word from the Holy Spirit—"Justice." He confided that he felt like he was letting me down because he had no amazing revelation or picture for me... just one word. He was hoping that the word was significant to me. I think I laughed out loud. That one word had tremendous significance to me! Of course I *did* share my testimony at that point! If I abide in Him and He abides in me then we *will* overlap. What felt like imagining to me was God showing me a current spiritual reality. Why "Justice" and why that night? I do not know. At the very least, I felt like God was challenging me to actually believe that we (He and I) are already one.

Spend some time (at least 15 minutes) dreaming with God, focusing on the aspects of heaven that you have a desire to experience. Submit your imagination to the Holy Spirit and simply imagine what it might look like to access those parts of heaven. If this is difficult, refer back to *Something to consider* **on page 12 and ask God to reveal any lie that you believe about your identity that may be affecting your experience of the atmosphere of heaven.**

Day 2

The Obedience of Faith

Please read chapter two again today. There's one more thing I want to examine in verse 2.

> *"[2]in which you formerly walked according to the course of this world, according to the prince of the power of the air, of the spirit that is now working in the sons of* ***disobedience****."*

> disobedience = G543 apeitheia—*disbelief* (obstinate & rebellious); unbelief, disobedience.

Interesting, yes? The word that has been translated disobedience actually means disbelief/unbelief.

Disobedience and unbelief are related…

Take a look at Hebrews chapters 3 and 4.

Hebrews 3 and 4 further shows that sin, disobedience and unbelief are related to each other, if not synonymous. Now, here in Ephesians, Paul seems to be differentiating between those who cannot help but be under the influence of the prince of the power of the air (unbelievers) and those that have other options (believers). Yet, there is a powerful Kingdom concept here that I don't want you to miss—**in whatever area you find disobedience you will also find some level of unbelief**.

Somewhere in the belief system that is involved with that issue there is misalignment, a crookedness of sorts, which must be aligned. The Holy Spirit is very good at making crooked things straight. When it comes to mindsets, He calls this process, "the renewing of the mind" (Romans 12:2).

Are there areas of your own life that lack the level of obedience to God that you desire?

Belief systems become hardwired into our brains—literally. Many of our beliefs about ourselves, God and others were learned early in childhood. They remain in operation in our lives (even wrong beliefs) unless those circuits are re-routed intentionally. The Holy Spirit knows exactly what must be re-routed. When we pray, "Help my unbelief," He will do exactly that, but rarely is it done without our active participation. The technique described in ***Something to consider*** from Week 1, Day 3 is one technique that can facilitate re-routing in the brain from unbelief/wrong-believing to right-believing.

"Immediately the boy's father cried out and said, I do believe; help my unbelief."

Mark 9:24

Spend some time (at least 15 minutes) surrendering your beliefs *in that area* to the Holy Spirit. Take responsibility for your lack of obedience and ask God to destroy its power in your life. Then ask Him to release His justice into the area of your life that has been affected. Invite Him to flood the eyes of your understanding *in that area* with His light, His truth. Pay close attention to anything He reveals to you. Record your experience.

Day 3

A Gift of God

Read chapter two again today.

What do you learn about the role of grace in your life from Eph 2:4-10?

Consider the relationship between these Scriptures:

> *"...for **all** have sinned and fall short of the glory of God" -Rom 3:23*
>
> *"For **by grace** you have been saved **through faith** and that not of yourselves, it is the gift of God, not as a result of works, so that **no one** may boast." -Eph 2:8-9*

We all start in the same place—Romans 3:23. Your faith activates the grace that saves you. The saving grace is a gift from God. The faith that activates the grace is also a gift from God. The significance in it not being a result of works is ***so that*** no one may boast. No one.

Huge Kingdom concept: any kind of grace is accessed by faith—and grace is always the gift of God *so that* no one may boast.

This is a beautiful protection provided by God for us that enables us to live a life of humility *if* we can grasp the understanding of the phrase "so that no one may boast."

> *"[10]For we are God's workmanship, created in Christ Jesus for good works, which God prepared beforehand so that we would walk in them."*

Why is it that we have no right to boast? Our individual, original design was created by God. Every good work we have done or ever will do was prepared for us in advance by God. He even strategically places the opportunities in our lives for accomplishing those good works *so that* we can walk in them. It's His grace that enables us to partner with His design—a design that is more fully accessed when we receive the gift of His righteousness and our minds are increasingly renewed. It's His grace that enables us to choose to perform any good work as well as enabling us to do the good work itself. My personal definition of grace is *God's power that enables*. Now, it is **you** who does the good work. **He enables *you*** to do the good work. This is why you can receive honor from men and give honor to men for a good work accomplished. Knowing that the desire to do the good work and the power to do the good work originated in God roots you in humility. Where there is humility there is no boasting.

What comes to mind, in your own life, as you meditate on grace (as the power that enables) & humility?

"In Him we have redemption through His blood, the forgiveness of our trespasses, according to the riches of His grace which He lavished on us..."

Ephesians 1:7-8

Can you pinpoint situations in your life where you can see that grace was enabling you to accomplish something that, perhaps previously, you were unable to accomplish?

Eph 1:8 showed us that His grace *has been* lavished on us. His grace is available to us 24 hours a day, 7 days a week. Sometimes the Holy Spirit gets your attention and points out the grace that is hovering over your situation, sometimes you take the initiative without a nudging from the Holy Spirit, and sometimes you stumble into grace before you even know you need it.

Record some examples of grace at work in or around your life and the way in which you became aware of the grace or the need for the grace.

Day 4

Good Works

Read chapter two.

We're not quite ready to leave verse 10. Yesterday we focused on the importance of realizing that the good things of God are always accomplished by grace. Today, I want to focus on those "good works" themselves. Verse 10 comes right out with it—you are created in Christ Jesus for good works.

"For we are His workmanship, created in Christ Jesus for good works, which God prepared beforehand so that we would walk in them."

Ephesians 2:10

What does that mean to you? How do you define "good works"?

Consider some things that Jesus had to say about His good works:

"My food is to ***do the will of Him who sent Me****, to accomplish His work." -John 4:34*

"I showed you many ***good works from the Father****, for which of them are you stoning Me?" -John 10:32*

"If I do not do ***the works of My Father****, do not believe Me." -John 10:37*

"I glorified You (Father) on the earth, having accomplished ***the work which You have given Me to do****." -John 17:4*

Now, this is what Jesus had to say about the works of those that would follow Him:

"Let your light shine before men in such a way that ***they may see your good works and glorify Your Father who is in heaven****." -Matt 5:16*

"...he who believes in Me, ***the works that I do, he will do also****. And greater than these he will do because I go to the Father." -John 14:12*

What do you learn from these verses?

How important is it that we “walk” in the good works that God has prepared for us?

From Matthew 5:16, did you catch the reason why it is important for you to accomplish good works AND for others to see those good works? Something about others seeing the good works causes them also to glorify God.

Record some good works that you know you have walked in (i.e. personal testimonies!)

Are there works that you know God has prepared specifically for you but have not yet been accomplished? If so, what’s stopping you?

Day 5

The Foundation

This is our last day to focus on chapter two. Please read through it one more time!

> **Focusing on verses 11-22, if you had to put a subtitle on this section, what would it be?**

Our understanding of the Kingdom of God hinges on our understanding of Jesus.

Mine might be "The Distance Traveled" or "Crazy Redemption". In that one salvation moment, we go from being totally outside the things of God to being totally immersed in God Himself. Paul's emphasis seems to be on our landing place. Remembering where we have come *from* puts us in a place of thankfulness and awe of saving grace, but **remembering where He has brought us *to* prepares us for our purpose on the earth**. A Kingdom mindset needs to understand both.

Consider verse 20:

> *"[20]having been built on the foundation of the apostles and prophets, Christ Jesus Himself being the corner stone..."*

> **What does this verse mean to you? How important is the foundation of a house? (Matthew 7:24-27 records Jesus' perspective on the importance of foundational material: rock vs. sand)**

Everything is built upon the foundation, but the cornerstone is crucial in the alignment of the foundation. Skew the cornerstone and things don't "square-up" or properly align. Our understanding of Jesus, the Cornerstone, determines our understanding of the apostolic and the prophetic which, in turn, sets the tone for the building that is being built. Our understanding of the Kingdom of God hinges on our understanding of Jesus.

Examine and consider the following verses. How do they each contribute to your understanding of Jesus?

"Jesus said to him, 'Have I been so long with you and yet you have not come to know me, Philip? He who has seen Me has seen the Father...'" -John 14:9

"You know of Jesus of Nazareth, how God anointed Him with the Holy Spirit and with power. He went about doing good and healing all who were oppressed by the devil, for God was with Him." -Acts 10:38

"...who, although He (Jesus) existed in the form of God, did not regard equality with God a thing to be grasped, but emptied Himself, taking the form of a bondservant, being made in the likeness of men." -Philippians 2:6-7

"He (Jesus) is the image of the invisible God..." -Colossians 1:15

"He (Jesus) is the radiance of His (Father God's) glory and the exact representation of His (Father God's) nature..." -Hebrews 1:3

So, when you hear the often quoted phrase, "Jesus is perfect theology," what do you think it means?

Still not convinced that our understanding is so important? Check out appendix B for a sample of Scriptures from the Old Testament that mention understanding and its importance to us all. Note: Appendix B is a subset of Scriptures that contain the Hebrew word *bene* (H955) which Strong's dictionary defines *to understand.*

Abundance

Week Three

♦Manifold Wisdom

♦Be Strengthened

♦The Dimensions of God-Love

♦Be Filled to the Fullness

♦Stay the Course!

Day 1

Manifold Wisdom

I would say read through chapter three today, but hopefully, the first thing you would notice is that the chapter starts off with "For this reason…" You have to go back and read chapter two so that you know the reason to which he is referring. Make sense? So it's chapter two and three today.

So, to what does "For this reason" refer?

Because we are being built up together, it is necessary that Paul reveal the mystery that has been hidden until now. The mystery of Christ: the Gentiles are fellow heirs and fellow members of His body and fellow partakers of the promise in Christ Jesus through the gospel. So the Jews had been the only heirs and doing a lot of work as the heirs. Now, the Gentiles were to be included. This reminds me of the parable of the laborers in the vineyard (Matthew 20:1-16). The laborers hired late in the work-day were paid the same amount as the laborers hired first. It doesn't seem fair to those who were hired first and did more work, yet it is a Kingdom core value—we don't receive anything from the Kingdom according to our work; we receive everything in the Kingdom according to our worth, which is defined through His worth and is tied only to our God-given identity. However, what we receive from the Kingdom will surely affect our work here on the earth.

"Is it not lawful for me to do what I wish with what is my own? Or is your eye envious because I am generous? So, the last shall be first and the first last."

Matthew 20:15-16

Verses 8-9 give the reader insight into part of Paul's calling or the purpose for "the grace that was given" to him."

What's the purpose for the grace?

One of the most significant statements in the entire New Testament:

> *"[10]...**so that** the manifold wisdom of God might now be made known through the church to the rulers and the authorities in the heavenlies."*

What is being made known? Who makes it known? To whom is the wisdom being made known?

Is this what it looks like in your own life? Would you agree that discerning God's wisdom on a matter is important? How can you apply this verse in a new way to your life?

Can you see an application in the world of intercession? How does this affect your understanding of the mechanics of intercession, if at all?

"...so that the manifold wisdom of God might now be made known through the church to the rulers and the authorities in the heavenly places."

Ephesians 3:10

Consider verse 13:

> *"[13]Therefore I ask you not to lose heart at my tribulations on your behalf, for they are your glory."*

What does this statement mean? What do you think it means for something that someone else experiences to "be your glory"?

It is unclear whether the original language states that "not losing heart" is their glory or the tribulations are their glory. Either way, Paul is focused on them not losing heart (staying the course, remaining in faith). We know this because of what he then asks from God on their behalf:

[14] For this reason (referring to verse 13)...

Second apostolic prayer:

"For this reason I bow my knees before the Father, [15]from whom every family in heaven and on earth derives its name, [16]that He would grant you, according to the riches of His glory, to be strengthened with power through His Spirit in the inner man, [17]so that Christ may dwell in your hearts through faith and that you, being rooted and grounded in love, [18]may be able to comprehend with all the saints what is the breadth and length and height and depth, [19]and to know the love of Christ which surpasses knowledge that you may be filled up to all the fullness of God."

This prayer is a familiar prayer. You have probably studied it, memorized it, and recite it periodically if not often. Tomorrow we will begin to break down Paul's request, verse by verse. But today:

Ask God to give you a fresh perspective on this prayer. Ask Him to give you fresh insight and then wait for His response. Record what you hear/see.

Day 2

Be Strengthened

Read chapter three today. We will pick up where we left off yesterday.

> *"[14]For this reason I bow my knees before the Father, [15]from whom every family in heaven and on earth derives its name, [16]that He would grant you, according to the riches of His glory, to be strengthened with power through His Spirit in the inner man, [17]so that Christ may dwell in your hearts through faith and that you, being rooted and grounded in love, [18]may be able to comprehend with all the saints what is the breadth and length and height and depth, [19]and to know the love of Christ which surpasses knowledge that you may be filled up to all the fullness of God."*

Referring back to verse 13, Paul doesn't want the Ephesians to lose heart because of his tribulations (he's writing from Rome while under house arrest) so he prays for them to be strengthened. This is not generic physical strength or mental strength, and it's not peace (pretty much our go-to whenever we need some sort of stability.) This strength is supernatural dunamis power that comes from the Holy Spirit straight into your inner man—it is spiritual strength.

Is there a limit to the amount of strength that can be granted? Only if there is a limit to the riches of God's glory.

Be strengthened with supernatural power *so that*

> *"[17]...Christ may dwell in your hearts through faith..."*

So, Christ dwelling in the heart by faith requires supernatural strength.

> **How do you reconcile this with the common understanding of "inviting Jesus into one's heart" as a salvation truth? Does He come and go? Could the emphasis be on "dwell"?**
> (Dwell = G2730 katoikeo— to house permanently; reside.)

"[17]...Being rooted & grounded in love..."

The type of love mentioned here is agape—it is unconditional love. It is not only God's love for you that is being emphasized here but God's *type* of love—it is the only love He knows.

- Rooted—all things come forth from God-love
- Grounded—God-love is what gives true stability and staying power

Can you recall life experiences in which God was rooting you in His type of love? Grounding you in His type of love? Can you see the difference?

"Abide in Me and I in you...he who abides in Me and I in him, he bears much fruit..."

John 15:4,5

Consider the attributes of God's type of love as listed below (1 Cor 13). Living a life that radiates God-love is a way of the Kingdom, a way of righteousness.

God-love is:

- Patient
- Kind
- Does not envy
- Does not boast/brag
- Is not arrogant
- Does not act unbecomingly
- Does not seek its own
- Is not provoked
- Does not take into account a wrong suffered (is not offended)
- Does not rejoice in unrighteousness
- Rejoices with the truth
- Bears all things
- Believes all things
- Endures all things

One thing to consider when meditating on the attributes of God-love is that the Holy Spirit is bringing each of us into alignment with these attributes. In other words, as we become like Jesus, we will each love in this manner.

> **Do you see evidence in your life that God has been at work in some of these areas? Is there one aspect of His type of love that He is currently highlighting in your life? What has been your process of transformation?**

Day 3

The Dimensions of God-Love

"But now faith, hope, love, abide these three; but the greatest of these is love."

1 Corinthians 13:13

Let's continue working our way through Paul's prayer. Please read chapter three again today.

Consider verse 18:

> *"[18]may be able to comprehend with all the saints what is the breadth and length and height and depth"*

It takes the supernatural dunamis power of God for us to be able to comprehend His type of love in all of its dimensions. It is a spiritual awakening. The word translated as comprehend in the NASB is the Greek word *katalambano* (G2638). It means to take eagerly, that is, seize or possess. It might have been more appropriate to translate it as "apprehend" rather than "comprehend."

> **Consider the four dimensions mentioned for God-love. Why four dimensions? Ask Holy Spirit for revelation on each one separately. Purposely submit your current understanding to Him and ask for alignment and increase. Record what you perceive.**

> *"[19]...To know (by experience) the love of Christ that surpasses (head) knowledge..."*

I added the words above in parenthesis to emphasize what Paul means here. We are wired to live out of experience/relationship/"be"ing. Head knowledge gives us something to compare experience with but it is not a substitute. Back in the garden of Eden, the tree of Life gave us an experience filled with Life, while the tree of knowledge left us empty and with the process of death at work within us.

Have you experienced this type of transition—from head knowledge to experiential knowledge? What was its effect on you? Did it draw you closer to Jesus?

Hopefully, it is becoming increasingly clear that it is God's desire that we experience Him. Wherever we lack experience in our relationship with Him lays an open invitation for us to position ourselves for that experience.

Are there aspects of the dimensions of God's type of love that you would like to experience? Today, spend some time asking God to take you from head knowledge to experiential knowledge of that dimension of His love. Ask Holy Spirit to give you Scriptures about that particular dimension of His love. His responses may surprise you! Meditate on those Scriptures. Jesus is the Word and He is the Door. Every Scripture is a door to an experience with God.

Day 4

Be Filled to the Fullness

Read chapter three today. Starting with verse 19,

> *"[19]...that you may be filled up to all the fullness of God."*

Does it surprise you to discover that experiencing the fullness of God is even possible? The fullness of God seems like something that might be reserved for Father God, Jesus and the Holy Spirit. Yet, Paul is asking God Himself to strengthen the Ephesians with supernatural dunamis power so that that they can be filled with the fullness of God. God walks the earth filled with humanity so that humanity can walk the earth filled with God. That is quite an inheritance for humanity!

"And then I will declare to them, 'I never knew you. Depart from Me, you who practice lawlessness.'"

Matthew 7:23

Is being filled with the fullness of God even something you can bring yourself to ask for? What, if anything, holds you back?

This week we have examined five results of being strengthened with supernatural dunamis power. Paul made this request so that the Ephesians would not lose heart, in other words, so that they would remain faithful, focused, and purposely Kingdom-minded. As crazy as it sounds, being strengthened with dunamis power is **not optional**. Christ dwelling in our hearts is not optional. Being rooted and grounded in God's type of love is not optional. Comprehending the dimensions of God-love is not optional. Experiencing the love of Christ is not optional. Being filled with the fullness of God is not optional. Why? Because we need every one of those things in order to remain faithful, and remaining faithful is not optional. We are being transformed into faithful people. He will finish what He started. It is our honor to partner with that process. Begin to pray this apostolic prayer over yourself, your family, your friends, and your sphere of influence **with a new understanding**.

I suspect that the fruit of this prayer is the main goal of every Christian's personal development—to be filled with the fullness of God is to finally have "Christ formed in us" (Galatians 4:19) or to be a "mature man" (Ephesians 4:13). To be filled with the fullness of God is the endgame to our personal development, but it is just *part* of your purpose on the earth.

Spend some time today in the presence of God. Specifically ask God if there is a lie that you believe about receiving His fullness? Use the technique from Week 1 to interact with God regarding anything that He reveals. Record your experience.

…so that they would remain faithful, focused and purposely Kingdom-minded.

Day 5

Stay the Course!

Today will be very simple. I want you to really think about what Paul has said so far in chapters 1-3. If you get anything out of this study I want it to be a fresh understanding of this letter as a whole. The Ephesians are prospering as believers and Paul seems to be giving them keys that will enable them to maintain their forward momentum.

Chapter 1: Live from your God-given identity and by the way, I pray God expands it!

Chapter 2: Remember where He found you? Now remember how dramatically He has changed you. Get the vision for where He is taking you.

Chapter 3: Don't lose heart no matter the circumstances—submerge yourself in God and live from that reality. Keep the vision of where you are headed before your eyes.

He's building toward something. Can you see it?

Meditate on your personal journey so far with God. Some questions to consider:

- **How dramatically has He changed you?**
- **Have you been given a specific personal vision of where He is taking you?**
- **Are there circumstances in your life, the lives of those around you, or in the world in general that seem to be closing in around you and causing you to nearly "lose heart"? In the midst of it all, are you keeping the vision of where God is leading you in view?**
- **What is God saying to you today?**

"Where there is no vision, the people are unrestrained..."

Proverbs 29:18

The Jigsaw Puzzle

Week Four

- ♦Unity
- ♦One Yet Many
- ♦Truth in Love
- ♦Dianoia
- ♦The New Self

Day 1

Unity

Read chapters 1-4 today as we begin to study chapter four.

Notice the chapter starts with "therefore." At the end of chapter three Paul was summing up an amazing prayer for the Ephesians by reminding them that God is able to do far more abundantly beyond what we ask or think. In other words, it may seem impossible that we can know God's type of love, and are so transformed by it that we only have that kind of love to give. And it may seem impossible that we can be filled to all the fullness with God—but He is absolutely able. Not only is God able to do it, we will need Him to so that we can move on to chapter four! Everything Paul talks about "doing" from here on out will hinge on you truly receiving His supernatural strength to live out of your God-identity and radiate God's type of love.

According to 4:2-3, what is "a manner worthy of the calling with which you have been called"?

In 4:3 Paul uses interesting language: "...preserve the unity of the Spirit in the bond of peace." We find some clear descriptors for the Spirit, which, of course, are also markers of the Kingdom.

When the Holy Spirit is involved, is it necessary to *establish* unity? How do you preserve it?

Do you understand the "unity of the Spirit" to be unity of *people* one with another or an individual's unity with the Spirit? Consider John 17:22-23.

"Peace I leave with you. My peace I give to you. Not as the world gives do I give to you..."

John 14:27

So, the unity of the Spirit is marked by peace.

Have you experienced this? If so, was it internal or external? Does that question surprise you?

If I were to paraphrase 4:3 in my own language I would write, "become conscious of your connection to the Holy Spirit; notice the peace that accompanies His presence. Remain in that awareness."

How would you paraphrase this Scripture?

Consider verses 4-6:

> *"[4]There is one body and one Spirit, just as also you were called in one hope of your calling; [5]one Lord, one faith, one baptism, [6]one God and Father of all who is over all and through all and in all."*

I could see how some might think this segment of Scripture suggests that there should not be the strong denominational division that is often experienced in the church. More importantly, it seems to clearly emphasize that in spite of any differences believers may have, we have some very significant things in common, and remembering the importance of these common things will keep us humble with each other and help us to preserve the unity of the Spirit.

What are your thoughts?

Become conscious of your connection to the Holy Spirit.

Paul has just emphasized the amazing things all believers have in common—the central things. Now he is about to make the point that we are different in the way God has gifted us. It's very similar to the passage in Corinthians where he says we are one body yet we each make up the different parts of the body—a hand is not a foot, an ear is not an eye, etc. It all starts with verse 7:

> *"[7]to each one of us grace was given according to the measure of Christ's gift."*

One interpretation of this Scripture is that everyone is given the grace they need in order to operate in whatever gift(s) God has given them, i.e. the type of gift determines the size or type of grace. Another interpretation might be that "the measure of Christ's gift" is referring to the gift of salvation or righteousness and therefore, the grace that is given is immeasurable, and we all have been given the same amount.

What do you think and why?

Day 2

One Yet Many

Read chapter four again today. We will focus on verses 11-13.

So, as the body of Christ we are one, yet each of us is a particular piece to the puzzle. There are five specific types of pieces that have a very important role found in verse 12:

> *"[12]for the equipping of the saints for the work of service, to the building up of the body of Christ..."*

In what way have you experienced each of these gifts equipping you for the work of service?

Apostle

Prophet

Evangelist

Pastor

Teacher

Verses 12 and 13 tell us that in our equipping we are being built up and heading toward something—a new reality:

> *"[13]until we attain to the unity of the faith, and of the knowledge of the Son of God, to a mature man, to the measure of the stature which belongs to the fullness of Christ."*

There's that phrase again—the fullness of Christ.

Taking some time to really think about your answer, do you think this is something that should or will take a lifetime to attain? Why or why not?

Day 3

Truth in Love

Read chapter four again today. Let's start with verse 14.

> *"[14]As a result, we are no longer to be children, tossed here and there by waves and carried about by every wind of doctrine, by the trickery of men, by craftiness in deceitful scheming."*

As a result of what?

Your God-given identity is uncovered and revealed to you in your experiential relationship with God.

There may be a subtle, underlying suspicion that truly being filled to all the fullness with God and walking out life in the reality of God's type of love is not something attainable until "we get to heaven," but those things are just the beginning of our lives here on the earth. It's not supposed to take a lifetime to learn how to love or to have the eyes of our understanding flooded with light.

Certainly love and understanding will continue to increase in our lives, for the duration of our lives, but there is something significant that we are to receive from our Father in heaven **that produces real transformation** in our lives early on. This transformation produces the reality of being filled to the fullness with God. We begin to have a living knowledge of the Son of God and start moving toward the measure of the stature, which belongs to the fullness of Christ. It's the foundation of living a life that administrates the Kingdom of God on the earth. Without it, we are "tossed here and there…"

Chapters 1-3 suddenly become very important. Everything that you do within the Kingdom of God flows from who you are—your God-given identity. Your God-given identity is uncovered and revealed to you in your experiential relationship with God. **There is no substitute**. Doing before becoming will not bring the full Kingdom result.

Have you experienced trying to "do" the work of the Kingdom without first "being" who the King says you are?

Let's look at verses 14, 15 and 16 together since it is all one thought:

> *"[14]As a result, we are no longer to be children, tossed here and there by waves and carried about by every wind of doctrine, by the trickery of men, by craftiness in deceitful scheming, [15]but speaking the truth in love, we are to grow up in all aspects into Him who is the head, Christ, [16]from whom the whole body, being fitted and held together by what every joint supplies, according to the proper working of each individual part, causes growth of the body for the building up of itself in love."*

At this point in the chapter, do you know what Paul means by "speaking the truth in love"?

The phrase "speaking the truth in love" is quite possibly one of the most misunderstood and abused phrases in our culture. It's often used as Scriptural support to justify one's attitude of correction toward another. Typically, there is very little love involved. In context, this is not at all what Paul is saying.

The meaning of the phrase "speaking the truth in love" is more fully revealed later in the chapter.

In the meantime, notice verse 16. When we are "fitted and held together by what every joint supplies, according to the proper working of each individual part" then growth comes to the whole body and it is built up in love.

Consider these Greek origins:

Fitted = G4883 sunarmologeo—to organize compactly

Held Together = G4822 sumbibazo—driven together, that is, united

Joint = G860 haphe—ligament as in fastening (that which attaches/fastens one to another)

Proper working = G1753 energia —efficiency or energy

Paraphrase verse 16 in your own language.

So, each of us **living out our individual part** (identity, purpose, power) and **properly being in relationship with and united to each other** (God-love) causes growth to come **to the whole body**. That means we each have a responsibility to the entire body of Christ to:

- Know who you are in Christ,
- Live out your God-given destiny
- Learn how to relate to all around you from the position of being rooted and grounded in God-love

We actually need who you are to emerge and radiate!

Spend some time soaking in the Presence of God. Intentionally connect to His Presence and soak in His light, asking Him to establish you in love and in light. Record your experience.

Day 4

Dianoia

"I pray that the eyes of your understanding may be enlightened..."

Ephesians 1:18 (KJV)

We are getting there! Read chapter four again.

Today we begin at verse 17, which, of course, starts off with "so this I say..." You know what that means—what he is about to say is related to what he has just said. I am focusing on these transitions because they are pivotal in the understanding of context. We have spent years taking blocks of Scripture out of their surroundings and (sometimes) applying them haphazardly. One result is that when we encounter them in context we don't actually read them in context —our brain sees a bunch of disconnected segments of Scripture and we read them as if they are separate from each other. No good!

Now, Paul has just made the point that we need each other. We need each other to be properly connected to God, which allows us to be properly connected to each other. He's also just said that it is time to grow up. What does "growing up" look like? It looks like the rest of chapter 4, 5 and most of 6!

Let's start at verse 17. Remember "dianoia" from Week 1 Day 4? It means "deep thought" or "that which enables understanding." At the beginning of the letter Paul asks God to "flood the eyes of their *dianoia* with light." Chapter 4:17-18 explain why that flooding of light is necessary and how it should distinguish us from the world around us.

> *"[17]...walk no longer just as the Gentiles also walk, in the futility of their mind, [18]being darkened in their understanding (dianoia), excluded from the life of God because of the ignorance that is in them, because of the hardness of their heart"*

Wow. A lack of understanding yields futility, exclusion from the Life of God, and hardness of heart. Notice Paul is advising them to no longer walk that way. In other words, **we are quite capable of living our lives with very little understanding and yielding very little fruit** (see Matthew 13:23), even as believers. Understanding in any area actually connects us to the Life of God in that area.

> **Is there any area in your life that is not yielding Kingdom fruit? Is pursuing God for understanding in this area something you are willing to do? If so, how will you do that?**

Continuing with verse 19:

> *"[17]...walk no longer just as the Gentiles also walk, in the futility of their intellect, [18]being darkened in their dianoia, excluded from the life of God because of the ignorance that is in them, because of their hardness of heart, [19]and they, having become callous, have given themselves over to sensuality for the practice of every kind of impurity with greediness."*

Verse 19 is more of a parenthetical to the actual point of this section of Scripture, but I would like to step out of context for a moment and ask you to take a look at Romans 1:18-32. It is basically a longer version of Ephesians 4:17-19.

In Ephesians 4:19, who does the "giving over"? In Romans 1:18-32, who does the "giving over"? What are your thoughts?

"Ask and it will be given to you; seek and you will find; knock and it will be opened to you."

Matthew 7:7

Day 5

The New Self

This is the last day to focus on chapter four. Please read it in its entirety.

In my opinion, we are now getting to the heart of this letter, verses 22-24:

> *"22...in reference to your former manner of life, you lay aside the old self, which is being corrupted in accordance with the lusts of deceit, 23and that you be renewed in the spirit of your mind 24and put on the new self, which in God has been created in righteousness and holiness of the truth."*

Everything so far has been leading up to this point—you are new so be new. There are three things Paul has just told them to do as a part of "growing up."

- Lay aside the old self
- Be renewed in the spirit of your mind
- Put on the new self

Think through the process of doing all three. Can you see the differences in each? To some degree, have you experienced these three realities? Were they "one time deals" or do you experience a cycle? Record some specifics.

What does being "renewed in the spirit of your mind" mean to you? What are some practical ways to accomplish this goal?

Paul now highlights some behaviors for those who are laying aside the old, changing their thinking and putting on the new. He begins in 4:24 and continues through 6:11. Oh yes, it's one long description of what relationship can look like when you live in your newness.

We will finish up today by focusing on the rest of chapter 4, verses 25-32. Let's start with verse 25:

> *"[25]Laying aside falsehood, speak truth each one of you with his neighbor, for we are members of one another."*

This verse is a quote from Zechariah 8:16:

> *"[16]These are the things which you should do: speak the truth to one another..."*

Considering both Ephesians 4:25 and Zechariah 8:16 (in context), what do you think Paul meant earlier in verse 15 by the phrase "speaking the truth in love"? Do you think his focus was on walking in the opposite of "deceitfulness, ...trickery...and craftiness", i.e. honesty, or on combating doctrinal issues?

According to Romans 12:2, renewing your mind should bring about transformation and that transformation reveals the will of God.

> *"[2]Do not be conformed to this world, but be transformed by the renewing of your mind so that you may prove what the will of God is..."*

As we consider verses 26-32, notice the transformation in behaviors.

- If/when anger comes, don't act on it; instead, get rid of it quickly.
- He who steals must not just stop stealing, but work with those same hands toward having enough to share with others.
- Not only guard your language, but go even further—only speaking things that edify others (encourage and build up) and be aware that your words carry grace to the hearers.

- Don't grieve the Holy Spirit.
- Let all bitterness, wrath, anger, clamor, slander and malice be put away from you. Instead, be kind, tender-hearted, and forgiving.

There is another Kingdom concept being revealed here. To illustrate this concept imagine a number line.

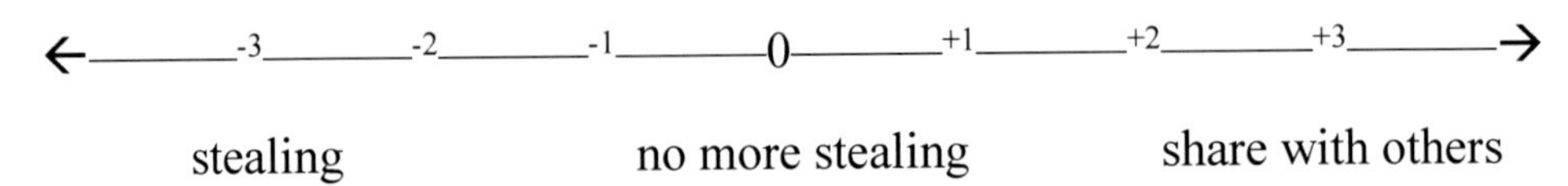

stealing | no more stealing | share with others

"I came that they may have life and have it abundantly."

John 10:10

Consider verse 28:

> *"28He who steals must steal no longer but rather he must labor, performing with his own hands what is good so that he will have something to share with one who has need."*

If stealing is a -3 on the number line, then "must steal no longer" would put you at zero. By stopping the wrong behavior, you have stopped sinning. But Paul doesn't stop there and neither did Jesus (Matt 5:20-48). Now, those same hands that used to take from others should be redeemed and used to do something that will enable you to give away to those who need it, which might put you at positive 3. Even just using those same hands to earn enough so that *you* don't need to steal would be "enough" from the world's perspective, right? At least you wouldn't be stealing. But the Kingdom marker is found in the dramatic redemption of those same hands. They are now to be used to give to others who may otherwise be tempted to steal. This is a very big deal! Those hands have not just stopped being the problem, **they have become part of the solution**.

The very next verse is another example of this principle.

> *"29Let no unwholesome word proceed from your mouth, but only such a word as is good for edification according to the need, so that it will give grace to the hearer."*

It is not enough to "let no unwholesome word proceed from your mouth." Simply stopping the negative talking is not the fullness of what is possible for your life. That very same mouth is to speak words that edify and release grace to the hearer for their need. Words that encourage and build up also release real supernatural power to the hearer to come into alignment with Heaven on earth in the situation.

The neutralizing of a problem is never the full manifestation of the Kingdom of God. This is one way we know that coping with an issue or with pain or with fear is never the endgame. We may find it necessary *in order to reach the endgame,* but coping in and of itself is not a manifestation of the Kingdom of God. It is the manifestation of the Kingdom of God that is **the very definition of God's will for your life.**

Verses 31 & 32 are yet another example of a transformation.

The Kingdom of God should bring more than enough into a situation. If more than enough has not manifested, then we have an opportunity, and perhaps even a responsibility, to work with the Holy Spirit until it does.

Can you identify things from your own life where the Kingdom of God came and the result was a dramatic 180 degree turn? Can you identify parts of your identity that have been transformed in this way?

Are there situations in your life or aspects of your identity where you now wonder if maybe the fullness of the Kingdom of God has yet to come? Maybe there is more than just getting to the zero mark. Maybe there is yet some Kingdom to experience in that area?

Spend some time in the Presence of God today talking to Him about that very thing. Ask Him to show you what it means for the fullness of the Kingdom to come in that area. And then ask Him how you can partner with Him to bring it to pass. Jot down your experience.

From the Kingdom

Week Five

- ♦Inheritance
- ♦The Kingdom is in the How
- ♦Relationship
- ♦Christ and the Church
- ♦One Flesh

Day 1

Inheritance

Today we begin chapter five. Paul continues to define "growing up". He begins the chapter with "therefore" so be sure to find out *what it is there for*.

In the process of transformation, as you put off the old ways and put on the new, you will continue to be faced with choices and opportunities. Staying on task will require focus.

> *"[1]Therefore be imitators of God, as beloved children [2]and walk in love, just as Christ also loved you and gave Himself up for you, an offering and a sacrifice to God as a fragrant aroma."*

Simple enough, right?

What does it mean to imitate God as a child? Rather than focusing on child-likeness, consider a father/child relationship in your answer. How does a young son or daughter imitate their dad?

When you relate to God, as a child would to a father, then you "do what he does". Recall Jesus' words in John 5:19: "I only do what I see My Father do..."

Doing what He saw His Father do was more than obedience. It was inheritance. In a parent/child relationship, obedience may be where it starts but as that relationship matures and understanding grows it becomes inheritance. Inheritance will only come one way—through being a son.

Imitating God has to do with your relationship with God, walking in love has to do with your relationship to others. God is continually showing us how to be lovers.

Verses 5-7 reveal what it looks like to *not* walk in your godly inheritance. As we found out earlier in this letter, it is quite possible to partner with these wrong

"...you have received a spirit of adoption as sons..."

Romans 8:15

behaviors as a believer, but it is not your inheritance. In fact, consider the following regarding verse 5:

> 5*For this you know with certainty, that no immoral or impure person or covetous man, who is an idolater, has any inheritance in the Kingdom of Christ and God.*

The verb translated as *has* in the verse above is the Greek word echo (G2192). So, you might say that one who partners with these ungodly behaviors does not echo inheritance in the Kingdom of God. In other words, that behavior does not come out of your Kingdom inheritance, so it must be coming from a previous inheritance – the one that belongs to the old you, the dead you. Verse 6 tells us that ungodly behavior is associated with the "sons of disobedience". And as we discovered in Week 2 Day 2, disobedience is related to unbelief. Before you believed in Jesus you were in a general state of unbelief and disobedience and were drawing from an inheritance rooted in death. According to Romans 8:16, The Spirit Himself bears witness that, as a new creation, you belong to a new family and have a new inheritance. You are learning how to draw from your godly inheritance, being renewed in the spirit of your mind.

How important is it for you to truly see Father God as a father and to be living out of His inheritance?

This takes us right back to chapter one and Paul's desire that the Ephesians would know the glory of God's inheritance. Our Kingdom inheritance looks like something. Not only does it look like something, it radiates something—it has a glory. Glory radiates, influences, affects those around us. More and more we are learning that living for God (emphasis on doing/obedience) may be where it started but living **from God** (emphasis on being/inheritance) is where it is headed.

Spend some time in the Presence of God asking Father God to fine tune your belief systems regarding Him as your Father. Use the exercise from Week 1 Day 3 to identify any wrong believing. You might want to ask Him if there is a lie you believe about Him as a Father.

Day 2

The Kingdom is in the How

Please read chapter five again today.

In verse 11 Paul exhorts us 'to not participate in the unfruitful deeds of darkness, but instead even expose them'. Some translations say, 'rebuke' or 'reprove'.

Is Paul talking about exposing others' deeds of darkness or your own? Whose behavior has he been focusing on throughout the entire letter?

Let's say Paul has changed his focus momentarily and is indeed exhorting us to expose others' deeds of darkness.

How do you approach the act of exposing darkness from a Kingdom mindset? Take into account v13 as well as Matthew 5:15:

"[13]But all things become visible when they are exposed by the light, for everything that becomes visible is light." –Ephesians 5:13

"[15]nor does anyone light a lamp and put it under a basket, but on a lampstand and it gives light to all who are in the house." –Matthew 5:15

When we expose darkness in the world around us or in others' behavior, we are not only exposing a thing to the light, we are exposing it ***by*** the light—thereby affecting change by *being* light (v8). Being light speaks to identity and behavior (the way in which you do a thing).

One example of non-Kingdom exposing might be accusation. Accusation can expose, but if accusation exposes darkness then what is it exposing darkness *to*? More darkness. Will darkness change darkness?

It is a Kingdom core value that **the end does not justify the means**. *How* we do what we do **matters**.

"You are the light of the world. A city set on a hill cannot be hidden."

Matthew 5:14

Have you experienced things in your life being exposed in a negative way? Have you exposed others' in a wrong way?

Alternatively, have you experienced a change in your life because you were exposed to the light in a way that was not accusatory or condemning?
Give some examples of exposing others in a right way, if there even is a right way.

Now, let's say Paul is exhorting us to take our own stuff, our own dark deeds, into the Presence of God and expose them to the light. Isn't this the same as confession of sin and the destruction of that record of sin by the One who is Light? Just the act of exposing your stuff *to* God brings transformation – out of darkness and into the light is powerful in the spirit realm.

Verse 14 furthers the point:

> *"[14]Awake sleeper and arise from the dead and Christ will shine on <u>you</u>."*

Dark deeds are rooted in fear and affect death. They came forth from a different inheritance; an inheritance from which you no longer want to operate.

Verse 14 is a quote from Isaiah 60:1-2. Check out what happens as a result of Christ shining on you according to Isaiah:

> *"[1]Arise, shine, for your light has come. The glory of the Lord has risen upon you. [2]For behold, darkness will cover the earth and deep darkness the peoples but the Lord will rise upon you. His glory will appear upon*

> *you. [3]**Nations will come to your light and kings to the brightness of your rising.**"*

God so wants to shine on us! But we will have to arise from the dead which means stepping out of the old identity and no longer drawing from an inheritance rooted in death as we put on the new identity and draw from our inheritance that is rooted in Life. His light or glory upon you will draw others into that light. He does not want the people in deep darkness to stay there. You are His magnet of light. He will draw nations and kings into your light and the people will be His reward. This is quite a plan. So…

> *"[15]...be careful how you walk, not as unwise men but as wise, [16]redeeming the time... [17]...do not be foolish but understand what the will of the Lord is."*

One last question for today: How does one redeem the time? Think big!

"Greater love has no one than this - that one lay down his life for his friends."

John 15:13

Day 3

Relationship

Read chapter five again today.

Paul continues to describe what growing up looks like – what relationship can look like once you have "put on the new". He also continues with the pattern of redemptive behavior. Notice the contrast:

Do		Don't
[1]imitate God, [2]walk in love	vs	[3]immorality, impurity, greed
[4]Give thanks	vs	[4]filthiness, foolish talk, coarse jesting
[15]Walk wise	vs	[15]be unwise
[16]redeem the time		
[17]understand the will of the Lord	vs	[17]be foolish
[18]be filled with the spirit	vs	[18]be drunk with wine [18]dissipation (lessening of who you are)
[19]speak to one another in psalms, spiritual songs		
[19]making melody in your hearts		
[20]always giving thanks		

And then comes the whopper in verse 21:

"[21]be subject to one another in the fear of Christ."

Why do I say it's the whopper? Because it begins a whole segment of Scripture that has the tendency to make many cringe. Let's investigate "be subject to".

G5293 hupotasso—to subordinate
from G5259 hupo—under
and G5021 tasso—arrange

So, you might say to "be subject to" is to "arrange yourself under". That definition sounds suspiciously like being a servant leader—serve one another (Gal 5:13), love one another (John 13:34), prefer others (Rom 12:10), bear one another's burdens (Gal 6:2), etc. It's definitely not incongruent with who Jesus was or the life He demonstrated for us.

Personal testimony

Our family had just moved into a new geographical area and we were in search of our new church home. My husband was fairly certain which church God was highlighting but I was unsure. Although we really connected with the senior pastors we had a hard time connecting to the church body. The atmosphere felt confrontational and I had no desire to fight a fight that God wasn't asking me to fight. One morning I was having an honest discussion with God. Had we chosen the wrong place? Why did I feel so uncomfortable if it was the right place for us? God's response totally surprised me. He asked me if I was willing to let the next few years be "not about me".

Being submitted to each other is a subset of loving each other with God's type of love.

For both my husband and I the previous three years had been about ministry training: how to operate in the gifts of the Spirit, heal the sick and prophesy. It had also been about establishing a Kingdom perspective within us. Now God was asking me if I could handle the next few years being about something else, some**one** else actually. He showed me the senior pastors of the church we had been attending and asked me if I would be willing to "come up under them and cause them to prosper". I had never heard that phrase before but as He spoke that phrase to me I understood that it was His definition of submission. In that moment it was the most beautiful thing I had ever heard. I was overwhelmed with His love for that couple. I could feel the weight of their assignment for the region and their importance to the heart of God. I never questioned our place there again. And I have never felt the same way about submission.

So, perhaps Kingdom submission is not so much about *the giving up* as it is about *accepting the honor*. Incorporating "cause to prosper" into the definition of submission helps us to see the concept from a Kingdom perspective. Being submitted to each other is a subset of loving each other with God's type of love.

Before we can wholeheartedly submit to each other, we really need to be saturated with His love for us. Hence, Paul's prayer leading up to this section – that we would experientially know God and His love. In some ways it's like a recipe for Kingdom life:

1. Make the exchange with Jesus—aspects of your old identity (led by a soul that houses the corrupt 'flesh' structure) in exchange for the corresponding aspect of your **true identity** (led by your spirit in submission to the Holy Spirit as Christ is formed in you)

2. Be submerged in the love of the Father—this brings aspects of renewal to your mind and transformation to your soul and body

3. Love others

4. Repeat steps 1-3

But there's more to this little bitty whopper of a Scripture:

"21 submit to one another ***in the fear of Christ****"...*

What does the fear of God have to do with it?

Read 1 Samuel 24:1-6 and Psalm 105:15 before you answer. Although the phrase "fear of the Lord" or "the fear of God" is not specifically used in these two examples, would you agree that seeing others through the lens of the fear of God is demonstrated?

Embracing the fear of the Lord has many benefits:

"The eye of the Lord is on those who fear Him." -Psalm 33:18

"The angel of the Lord encamps around those who fear Him." -Psalm 34:7

"Surely His salvation is near to those who fear Him that glory may dwell in our land." -Psalm 85:9

"For as high as the heavens are above the earth, so great is His lovingkindness toward those who fear Him." -Psalm 103:11

Ask the Holy Spirit if there is some cleaning up to be done in your understanding of submission. Go where He leads you. If you start remembering past experiences then imagine each one as separate pieces of paper. Individually, take responsibility for the experience—for your role in it, if any, but more importantly for accepting what it taught you. Then lay that experience (piece of paper) before Father God. Make a pile! When you are done adding to the stack, release it to Him. See yourself take a few steps back from the pile to demonstrate your release and repentance. Now ask Father God what He would like to do with that stack. Ask Him if He has something in exchange for you that will renew your mind with a better understanding of submission. Record your experience.

Day 4

Christ and the Church

Hopefully, the exercise from yesterday has brought you into a place where you can take a fresh look at submission and its role in relationships. Read through chapter five.

I suspect many misunderstandings and harsh perspectives on Ephesians 5:22-33 could have been avoided if verse 32 had been the opener to this segment of Scripture. Verse 32 reveals that the most important point Paul is making regarding submission and love has to do with Christ and the church. Oh, and by the way, it similarly applies to family.

So, we are going to begin by taking a look at this segment of Scripture with our focus on what Paul is saying specifically about Christ and the church.

> *"[22]Wives, be subject to your own husbands, as to the Lord. [23]For the husband is the head of the wife, <u>as</u> Christ is also the head of the church, He Himself being the Savior of the body."*

The word translated as "head" is the Greek word *kephale* (G2776). The vast majority of its usage in the New Testament is for the literal, physical head as a part of the human body. The word for "Savior" is *soter* (G4990) and is derived from *sozo* (G4982). *Sozo* means to save, heal, deliver and protect. *Soter* is one who provides saving, healing, deliverance and protection.

Paul seems to be relating Christ being the head of the church to Christ being the Savior (Healer, Deliverer, Protector). In other words, whatever he means by "head" is clarified by the understanding of Savior. We tend to read "head of the church" and think that it is referring to Him being in charge. But perhaps that's not Paul's emphasis here in this passage. Christ's role as Savior is not about being in charge – it's about submission to Father God, self-less love towards us, making a way for us to be drawn into the fullest and healthiest expression of life. Christ being the Savior makes way for us to be saved; being the Healer makes way for us to be healed; being the Deliverer makes way for us to be delivered; being the Protector makes way for us to be protected.

Consider Colossians 1:17-18 (KJV):

> *"[17]He is before all things and in Him all things hold together. [18]He is the head of the body... the beginning, the firstborn from the dead that He might be first in all things."*

Here in his letter to the Colossians Paul is emphasizing the firstness of being the head. As the head, Jesus is the first, the source and from where it all flows.

As Savior, He is the provision of our salvation and from where it all flows. So, when Paul describes Christ as the head of the church in Ephesians he seems to be emphasizing Him being the forger of our salvation as well as the one from whom salvation flows. Now, when you apply that concept to the husband in a family you get a man who forges ahead, making a way for his family and in the making of that way also releases all that is necessary for his family to follow. You might also define that man as a leader—quite an extraordinary leader.

Now, as a woman who has received the gift of righteousness from Jesus and as part of the church, I choose to come up under Jesus. I submit myself to Him as Lord but I also intentionally submit myself to Him as my Provider—provider of salvation, healing, deliverance, protection, etc. I also intentionally submit to Him as The Way so I follow Him in the way that He has made incorporating all of what He provides as I follow.

That is at least part of the picture Paul seems to be painting of the way submission works in the Kingdom of God. So, if I want it to be on earth as it is in Heaven (Matthew 6:10) then I should apply that same concept to my relationship with my husband. He is forging a way for our family and if I will arrange myself under him and come into agreement with the way he chooses to go with my own heart being intent on making him prosper then we will begin to look like the Kingdom.

Take 10 minutes to think of an example where either you, or a person you know, chose to arrange themselves under their husband with the intent to make him prosper? What did this look like?

Now that's just my part. Let's take a look at his part.

"[25]Husbands, love your wives, just as Christ also loved the church..."

How did Christ love the church?

"[25]...gave Himself up for her."

In the original Greek, that phrase "gave Himself up" or any variation of it that happens to be in your translation, does not mean laid His life down. It literally says that He yielded it up. He submitted His life to His Father as a demonstration of love for the church. Yielding up is an expression of love. It's an expression of His love for His Father and His love for us. Yielding up His life did indeed lead to Him laying down His earthly life on our behalf but it started with yielding up. Why would He do that?

"[26]so that He might sanctify her (the church) having cleansed her by the washing of water with the Word [27]that he might present to Himself the

church in all her glory, having no spot or wrinkle or any such thing but that she would be holy and blameless."

Jesus yielding up His life to the Father makes a way for us (the church) to be sanctified, cleansed, and brought into alignment with our new creation selves. A husband yielding up his life to his Father will have a similar effect. Yielding up his life to God will look like laying it down for his wife and will have a cleansing effect on her and the rest of his family.

Have you seen this done well? Was there a noticeable result within the family?

So, there is a cycle: submission from a place of love toward a spouse who submits himself to God from a place of love which yields sacrificial living out of love. Repeat. The effect of a lifetime of Greek thinking may pressure you to break it down linearly and ask the question: which comes first, the chicken or the egg, i.e. submission or sacrificial love? Hebrew thinking sees the circle and the dimensionality- they work together. One draws forth the other.

Now, it seems easier to submit to Jesus than to my husband because Jesus is the wisdom of God, He is love, He is the epitome of a servant King and has no selfishness in him. I can trust Him to make the "right" way and I can trust Him to provide all that I need. My husband is trying to figure it all out just like me. We're full of places that need to be healed and have many good intentions. My "arranging myself under" and his "yielding up" are works in progress. But, as we walk through life together and are increasingly living out of our newness, this cycle becomes easier and more natural. We are experiencing moments that look like the Kingdom—filled with righteousness, peace and joy. Those moments are extraordinarily beautiful. And the moments are beginning to extend into stretches of time.

There's a Kingdom dynamic that kicks in when one lays down their "life" for another. When I notice my husband authentically putting aside his own preferences or desires without offense, it draws out a desire within me to do whatever I can do to make him prosper. A cycle of life starts to gain momentum and I can begin to understand the cycle I see happening before the throne of God in Revelation 4:10. The 24 Elders throw down their crowns before the throne of God only to have them appear on their heads again… so they throw them down only to have them appear on their heads again. Groundhog Day in the throne room of Heaven! When we release back to God the glory He has put within us He only gives us more—a Kingdom pattern. One way Jesus released back to His Father the glory that had been put in Him was to offer Himself as a sacrifice for us. We see Him doing this and it draws out a desire within us to submit ourselves to Him and be the person He created us to be to make His Kingdom prosper.

> **Have there been times in your life when you found yourself in this cycle – either with God, with a spouse or even amid working relationships? Slices of time when relationship flowed in a healthy way and leadership through love made way for authentic "coming up under"?**

Day 5

One Flesh

Read chapter five one more time.

It's possible that yesterday was difficult. If you have had unhealthy experiences with submission in family life or in the church then it can be hard to see the concept positively at all. If it was a difficult day then please don't give up on seeing submission from a new perspective. Continue to bring the concept to your Father in Heaven until you feel a change in your perspective. He is the one who has made a way for your ways of understanding to be flooded with light. Pursue Him in that area until your way of understanding is flooded with light!

"...our old self was crucified with Him..."

Romans 6:6

Today we will focus on verses 28-33.

> *"[28]So husbands ought also to love their own wives as their own bodies. He who loves his own wife loves himself [29]for no one ever hated his own flesh but nourishes and cherishes it,* ***just as Christ also does the church****, [30]because we are members of His body. [31]FOR THIS REASON A MAN SHALL LEAVE HIS FATHER AND MOTHER AND SHALL BE JOINED TO HIS WIFE AND* ***THE TWO SHALL BECOME ONE FLESH****. [32]This mystery is great but I am speaking with reference to Christ and the church. [33]Nevertheless, each individual among you also is to love his own wife even as himself and the wife must see to it that she respects her husband."*

So, from verses 29 & 30 we glean that Christ loves, nourishes and cherishes the church. Where's the condition that the church must be mature, holy, and blameless before Christ will love her? Oh, that's right, we learned yesterday that it is Christ's love that actually enables the church to become mature, holy and without spot.

Does Jesus love in order to obtain a result or does His love simply produce a result? Can you see the subtle difference between the two realities?

Consider your attitude towards "the church" at large. Is it unconditional love? Is there a, "yes, but..." phrase that is part of your answer?

Previously, I quoted verse 30 as it appears in the NASB. I was a little surprised to discover that the NASB truncated the verse. There is more to it in the original language. The KJV translation expresses it like this:

> *"[30]For we are members of his body, of his flesh, and of his bones."*

Verse 31 is a quote from Genesis 2:24. Here is how Genesis 2:23-24 reads:

> *"[23]The man said, "this is now bone of my bones and flesh of my flesh. She shall be called Woman because she was taken out of Man". [24]For this reason a man shall leave his father and his mother and be joined to his wife. They shall become one flesh."*

There is way more here than meets the eye. Paul is relating the creation of Eve from within Adam to the creation of the church from within Christ. And the use of "flesh" is very significant. When you were born into this world you were born as part of the race of Adam, into his "flesh". You were "of Adam". When you were born from above or by the Spirit then you were born afresh into a brand new race. When Paul insists throughout his letters that you are a new creation he is not suggesting you think *as if* you were a new creation. You *are* a new creation. Jesus was the first—He was the first born of many (Romans 8:29). He came as the last Adam in order to accomplish what no one within that race could (Romans 8:3)—be without sin and become the sacrifice for sin itself. He left as the first born of many, leaving a way to follow and a legacy for us to step into. Part of our process of "growing up" includes leaving the identity that came from our old race behind and stepping into the new race of mankind. We are flesh of His flesh and bone of His bones. Becoming "one flesh" with Him is yet another invitation to step into oneness with Him. This is not sexual at all—**it's identity**.

Any additional insight in being flesh of His flesh? Bone of His bones? Consider Luke 24:39 and John 19:36.

Extra Credit: Have some extra time today? Try reading through Romans 8 with a new definition of "the flesh". Whenever you see that phrase think "fallen Adamic nature which is soul led" and when you see "according to the Spirit" or "in the Spirit" think "new creation nature – in Christ and spirit led". Does that bring a fresh understanding of that chapter?

All Things New

Week Six

- ♦Growing Up
- ♦As to the Lord
- ♦Stand Firm
- ♦The Armor: The New You
- ♦Peace, Love, Grace

Day 1

Growing Up

Welcome to Week six. The chapter number changed but the theme did not. We are still in the middle of relationship reboot and still learning what it means to grow up individually and corporately.

Read through the entire letter if possible today.

At the end of chapter five, Paul was overlaying a Kingdom picture of relationship between Christ and the church over the topic of marriage. He's now overlaying it over a few other types of relationships here in chapter six.

Verses 1-4 deal with the parent/child relationship.

> *"[1]Children, obey your parents in the Lord, for this is right. [2]HONOR YOUR FATHER AND MOTHER (which is the first commandment with a promise), [3]SO THAT IT MAY BE WELL WITH YOU AND THAT YOU MAY LIVE LONG ON THE EARTH. [4]Fathers, do not provoke your children to anger, but bring them up in the discipline and instruction of the Lord."*

We see from verses 1-3 that honor releases Life. Honoring that which has come before you causes you to enter into a cycle of life—honor is a "way". You honor because of who you are and the Kingdom that you are from.

Again, the Scripture quoted above is from the NASB translation. The last half of verse 4 in some other translations read:

> *"[4]... bring them up in the nurture and admonition of the Lord." –KJV*

> *"[4]... rear them tenderly in the training and discipline and the counsel and admonition of the Lord." –Amplified*

When I researched the original Greek for "discipline" and "instruction" (using the NASB as a guide) I discovered something interesting. The root for one was tutorage as you might expect, a clear relationship to discipling. The second word, when looking at the root, was a compilation of two concepts: "to place" and "to know". I realize that one can overexamine a thing and totally distort the original intent. So, rather than do that, I will suggest, that at the very least, within your understanding of "discipline and instruction" you leave room for "lead them in such a way as to **place** them into experiential **know**ledge of the Lord".

Are you starting to get a feel for what Paul is doing in this teaching on relationship in general? He's not just giving a "to do" list, he is giving the how or, more specifically, the way in which it is done. There is a way to do a thing that springs forth from death and a way that springs forth from Life. You are continually choosing **a source** by the way in which you do a thing—between Life and death. God's words from Deuteronomy 30:19 echo still.

> *"... I have set before you life and death, the blessing and the curse. So, choose life in order that you may live... "*

One part of growing up in Christ is to recognize that there is a choice being made. Another part is to choose the way that it is rooted in Life.

> **Can you identify times in your own life where you did a right thing but it was done in a way that was rooted in death (fear, control, anger) rather than Life (faith, love, hope)? Can you see the difference? Jot down a few examples of right things done in a wrong way as well as wrong things done in a right way.**

Day 2

As to the Lord

Let's tackle this last bit of teaching on relationship—slaves and masters. Verses 5-9 laid a foundation for many in the Civil War era (1861-1865) to believe that God was promoting slavery, or at least not *specifically* denouncing it. It may be hard for us to understand that way of thinking from this side of the timeline but if you approach this section of Scripture with the revelation that Jesus came to set us free *from* slavery to sin and death and by doing that He was condemning the "way" of slavery then this section of Scripture takes on new life.

"So if the Son makes you free, you will be free indeed."

John 8:36

> *"[5]**Slaves** (G1401), be obedient to those who are your **masters** (G2962), according to the flesh, with fear and trembling, in the sincerity of your heart, as to Christ; [6]not by way of eyeservice, as men-pleasers, but as **slaves of Christ**, doing the will of God from your heart (G5590). [7]With good will render service, as to the Lord, and not to men, knowing that whatever good thing each one does this he will receive back from the Lord, whether slave or free. [9]And masters, do the same things to them and give up threatening, knowing that both their Master and yours is in Heaven, and there is no partiality with Him."*

If you are using a translation other than NASB, you may have noticed slightly different wording. Let's take a look at some Greek origins from Strong's.

> G1401 doulos—from deo (G1210) which means to bind; a *slave* (literally or figuratively, involuntarily or voluntarily; frequently therefore in a qualified sense of *subjection* or *subserviency*):—bond (-man), servant.

> G2962 kurios—*supreme* in authority, that is, (as noun) *controller*; by implication *Mr.* (as a respectful title):—God, Lord, master, Sir

Many translations prefer servant or bondservant to slave. Notice the definition includes voluntary or involuntary. Biblically, a bondservant was someone who voluntarily served a particular person or family and in that way was bound to them. A slave is one who is involuntarily bound to serve another. The main point Paul is making is the way in which one serves: with fear and trembling (of God), in sincerity of heart, doing the will of God from your soul, and with good will. He goes on to say that the ones who are in authority are to "do the same thing" and give up threatening—that seems to parallel the idea of choosing not to operate out of fear or use fear as a tactic, but to be rooted and grounded in love. And we know these principles apply to us all in most situations in which we find ourselves. The way we do a thing as a spouse, as a parent, as a child, as an employee or as an employer matters. At the heart of Kingdom living, it is the way we do a thing that will reveal our new nature. The thing that we do is also very important but *the way* is key. Living life rooted in the love of God for us and releasing that love as a way of relating to others will certainly be one way the world will be drawn to our light.

"They shall eat of the fruit of their own way and be satiated with their own devices."

Proverbs 1:31

Why do you think Paul specifically uses servant language? Ask the Holy Spirit for insight and record your thoughts.

Day 3

Stand Firm

Today we transition into the summary of Paul's letter to the Ephesians. He began by acknowledging their faith and love and continues by exhorting them to continue the process and grow up into the fullness of who they are, the fullness of their new nature. Please read chapter six.

Earlier, in chapter three of the letter, Paul prays,

> *"[16]that He would grant you, according to the riches of His glory to be strengthened with* ***dunamis power*** *through His Spirit in the inner man."*

What Paul has laid out for the Ephesians as well as you and I will take supernatural power to accomplish. This explosive power is required for a very real repositioning of ourselves from living out of an old identity into living from our new identity and supernatural inheritance. We will not have the luxury of our souls leading us. We will have to learn how to live this new life with our spirits leading us. It is through our spirit that His Spirit releases His dunamis power. Our repositioning will enable us to live life in relationship with God and with others differently—in a manner worthy (Ephesians 4:1).

> **Have you experienced any degree of shifting from being soul-led to being spirit-led? Have you developed ways to discern which state you are in?**

Now Paul says,

> *"[10]Finally, be strong in the Lord and in the strength of His might."*

It is through this same spirit-to-Spirit connection that God releases the strength of His might. Explosive dunamis power moves things, but might will give you the supernatural strength to remain. Remain in what? Remain in your new identity (in Christ) being led by your spirit (submitted to His Spirit) and drawing from your godly inheritance.

> *"[11]Put on the full armor of God so that you will be able to stand firm against the schemes of the devil. [12]For our struggle is not against flesh and blood but against the rulers, against the powers, against the world forces of this darkness, against the spiritual forces of wickedness in the heavens."*

Paul reminds us that the armor is not to protect us from people but from spiritual forces.

Why is this distinction so important? What are the two most important commandments to followers of Jesus?

We stand firm in God's ways so as to resist dark ways.

Love God and love others—with God's type of love. How will that ever be possible unless we really do become like Him? Telling His story is not necessarily the same as becoming like Him. Becoming like Him is how the world will know He was exactly who He said He was and was sent by our Father (John 17:21). It will be what draws the ones still in darkness to the ones radiating light.

We are not standing firm against *people*, but first and foremost we are standing firm against **schemes**. In Greek it is the word methodeai. There is no surprise in the definition. We stand firm against the methods of darkness. You might say we stand firm in God's ways so as to resist dark ways. The *way* in which we do a thing matters. It might very well be the main thing in the process of our lives.

The Scripture goes on to say that we are also standing firm against rulers, powers, world forces of darkness and spiritual forces of wickedness in the heavens. Of course, these are the entities that are devising the schemes. These are spirit beings which is why we need "the strength of His might" in our spirits. Their schemes can be powerful but they lose a bit of their oomph when we truly realize that they are just schemes. It is all trickery—wooing us into partnership with dark ways. Their target is your soul.

Their schemes are designed to lure your soul. When we are positioned rightly, abiding in Him as an identity and **being led by our spirit** then these schemes are devised to get us to *move*: move from being spirit-led back to being soul-led. The strength of His might enables us to remain—remain in our true identity, being led by our spirits, rooted and grounded in love, and living in the way of love with those around us. Sometimes, oftentimes, this "remaining" seems to be moment by moment.

Now, if you are *not* positioned rightly, having not yet made the transition from old to new, then the schemes are designed to prevent you *from* moving. The strength of His dunamis power will be what gets you through the transition. The transition from being mostly soul led to being spirit led is a process. It takes time, intentionality, and explosive supernatural power. You functioning in Christ is one of Satan's nightmares. Us all functioning in Christ is his worst nightmare. He has no defense against our unity in Christ.

Identify some ways in which your soul gets caught in the snares of the enemy. Be real - what trips you up? It may be easy to identify the big things and maybe you have already dealt with many big things but what about the little things? Those little things may be the deadliest. Those traps are subtle and often go undetected, masquerading as '"the way God made me" kind of stuff. Whatever the trap, can you identify the scheme at work to get you into the trap?

Day 4

The Armor: The New You

Ephesians chapter six is known as the part of the Bible that gives us the description for the "Armor of God". Our children learn it in Sunday School and prayer warriors are taught to "put it on" before entering the battle of intercession. But what if chapter six is not so much an independent description of the armor but rather the picture of the armor presented here is a summary of all Paul has described in the previous five chapters? Then the armor of God is not something you put on during prayer as much as it is a visual used to describe the way you live your life. The armor of God is a picture of you as a new creation.

Let's take a look at the armor described in 6:14-17.

> *"[14]Stand firm therefore, having girded your loins with truth and having put on the breastplate of righteousness, [15]and having shod your feet with the preparation of the gospel of peace. [16]In addition to all, taking up the shield of faith with which you will be able to extinguish all the flaming arrows of the evil one. [17]And take the helmet of salvation and the sword of the Spirit which is the word of God."*

So, "gird your loins with truth". Truth is to cover your loins.

What is the significance of loins?

The armor of God is a picture of you as a new creation.

It is the place of reproduction. You reproduce your own DNA—in other words you reproduce *who you are*. What you believe is the truth that you will reproduce.

There seem to be several elements to the meaning of truth here.

- The first element is integrity—the way of truthful living. As we saw in Chapter three, integrity is a Kingdom "way".

- The second element is truth in terms of what we have learned through life experience mostly from childhood—our belief systems. We live according to those belief systems, many times unaware of the underlying beliefs. This element of truth begins to overlap with the next.

- The Word of God as revealed by the Spirit of Truth and the Spirit of Understanding.

Part of our transition from old to new is our exchanging the wrong beliefs (or lies) for right beliefs (the revealed Word of God). The Holy Spirit seems to be continually replacing our "truth" with His Truth. After all, He is the Spirit of Truth (John 14:17; John 15:26; John 16:13). In terms of identity, Jesus is the Truth (John 14:6) and we are one with Him. The degree to which we live from *that* reality will be the depth of the Kingdom that we have the capacity to reproduce.

"[14] ...Put on the breastplate of righteousness..."

Why a *breastplate* of righteousness? What does the breastplate protect?

Read Ezekiel 36:24-27 and Hebrews 8:10-13. As part of the New Covenant God has promised to give us a new heart and write His laws upon that new heart. This is His work. Jesus gives us the gift of His righteousness and in doing so becomes our righteousness (1Corinthians 1:30)—identity! Our new heart, encoded with the laws of God within the New Covenant, goes hand-in-hand with our new righteousness. Without the righteousness of God our new heart would be destined for stone once again.

"[15] ...having shod your feet with the preparation of the gospel of peace."

Feet seem to have importance to Jesus.

- "*Whoever does not receive you, nor heed your words, as you go out of that house or that city,* ***shake the dust off your feet***." *-Matthew 10:14*

- "*Turning toward the woman He said to Simon, 'Do you see this woman? I entered your house and you gave me* ***no water for my feet*** *but she has* ***wet my feet with her tears and wiped them with her hair***.'" *-Luke 7:44*

- "*But the father said to his slaves, 'Quickly bring out the best robe and put it on him and put a ring on his finger and* ***sandals on his feet***." *-Luke 15:22*

- "*Then He poured water into the basin and began to* ***wash the disciples' feet*** *and to wipe them with the towel with which He was girded...* ***He who has bathed needs only to wash his feet, but is completely clean***..." *-John 13:5, 10*

- John the Baptist seemed to understand the significance of feet when he said, "*As for me, I baptize you with water but One is coming who is mightier than I and* ***I am not fit to untie the thong of His sandals***..." *-Luke 3:16*

Any insight regarding the significance of feet? Why is peace paired with feet? And finally, why the "<u>preparation</u> of the gospel of peace" and not just "the gospel of peace"?

And, of course, Jesus is our peace (Eph 2:14)—identity.

> *"16 ...taking up the shield of faith with which you will be able to extinguish all the flaming arrows of the evil one."*

So the shield of faith is to extinguish the flaming arrows **keeping them from ever touching you**.

Is this your experience? What is a flaming arrow?

"He who dwells in the shelter of the Most High will abide in the shadow of the Almighty."

Psalm 91:1

Can I blow your mind? The word translated as shield is the Greek word thureos (G2375). It's derived from thura (G2374) which means "door", as in,

> *"I am the door; if anyone enters through Me he will be saved and will go in and out and find pasture." –John 10:9*

Thura also means portal. Strong's dictionary actually says that the shield is "large and door shaped". You stand behind that large door-shaped shield. Your shield is a little more than a shield. Your shield is a physical representation of a gateway—a door into the heavenly realms. Faith gets you through the door. No flaming arrows in that realm. Oh, the riches of the glory of His inheritance! When you live from that realm, you are truly living from your new identity.

Consider Jesus' prayer in John 17:

> *"24Father, I desire that they also, whom You have given Me, be with Me where I am so that they may see My glory..."*

So we have a clear invitation from Jesus Himself to "go in and out" and "be with Him where He is". This revelation makes me forget about those arrows. The King James translation expresses the flaming arrows as "fiery darts". We have a portal and a sword, the enemy has schemes and darts. Enough said.

Jesus is the door (John 10:9) **and** the shield (Genesis 15:1; Psalm 3:3; Psalm 28:7)—identity!

Continuing with verse 17:

"17 ...take the helmet of salvation..."

What does a helmet protect?

Why is protecting our minds with "salvation" important?

Maybe the helmet isn't for protection necessarily... maybe it's the overlay for the mind—a new way of thinking, perhaps a *renewed* mind. A renewed mind brings transformation. Actually, it brings transfiguration (Romans 12:2), same word for both. Yes, think Jesus on the mountain with Peter, James and John AND Moses and Elijah—that same kind of transfiguration. Now that I think about it, that whole scenario in Mark 9 was rather portalish, don't you think?

And of course Jesus is our salvation (Exodus 15:2; Psalm 27:1; Psalm 62:1)—identity! According to Psalm 140:7, He also covers your head during battle.

That's a good place to stop for the day. Have fun meditating on Jesus being a portal. And as you do, consider Psalm 23:5 in a whole new light:

"You prepare a table before me in the presence of my enemies..."

Remember, the flaming arrows (or fiery darts) come from the evil one. Your enemies are not flesh and blood, they are spiritual. The evil one motivates and supplies your enemies. When the flaming arrows are flying, Jesus prepares a table for you. What if the table is in a heavenly realm or, to clarify, a dimension distinct from where the arrows are flying?

Day 5

Peace, Love, Grace

Let's finish up Chapter six. Please read it one last time.

We will pick up where we left off yesterday—the last piece of the armor.

> *"[17] ...and the sword of the Spirit which is the word of God."*

There are some interesting discoveries to be made in this second half of verse 17. First, the word translated as sword is machaira (G3162). It means a knife or a dirk. It is distinctly different from the sword that appears coming out of Jesus' mouth in Revelation 1:16. That sword is more of a sabre. And the word of God here is the *rhema* of God, as opposed to the *logos*. The difference between logos and rhema is a significant study all on its own. The Greek definitions don't help very much. I think the best way to truly understand the difference is to study them both in context through a thorough word study—which is more than just one day's homework. Here are a few cliff notes:

Logos, G3056

- *In the beginning was the Logos, the Logos was with God and the Logos was God. He was in the beginning with God. All things came into being through Him and apart from Him nothing came into being that has come into being. -John 1:1-3*
- *And the Logos became flesh and dwelt among us and we saw His glory, glory as of the only begotten from the Father, full of grace and truth. -John 1:14*
- *He is clothed with a robe dipped in blood and His name is called the Logos of God. -Revelation 19:13*

Rhema, G4487

- *It is the Spirit that gives Life; the flesh profits nothing. The rhemas that I have spoken to you are spirit and are Life. -John 6:63*
- *Man shall not live by bread alone but on every rhema that proceeds out of the mouth of God. -Matthew 4:4*
- *Faith comes by hearing and hearing by the rhema of Christ. -Romans 10:17*

So, based on the sword of the Spirit being the rhema of God as described in the above Scriptures, is this a destructive sword? For offense or defense?

What are some purposes for the Sword of the Spirit?

*"18 ...pray at all times **in the spirit...**"*

How do you understand praying "in the spirit"? Why do you believe this?

Now we come to the end of the letter. Notice that Paul writes,

> *"23 Peace be to the brethren, and love with faith, from God the Father and the Lord Jesus Christ. 24 Grace be with all those who love our Lord Jesus Christ with incorruptibility."*

Interestingly, he does *not* write, 'I pray that God would grant you peace, love and grace…'. Can you see the difference? He seems confident that he is able to release God's grace and peace *at will*. Paul consistently writes like this in the introduction and conclusions of his letters.

How confident are you that you are able to release God's grace and peace *at will*? What does "freely you have received, freely give" (Matthew 10:8) mean to you?

Conclusion

Flooded with LIGHT

The Ephesians' faith and love were notable; it was a very good start. But there was more for them a there is more for us. We are growing up—realizing that schemes have kept us busy living from the wro identity, longing for purpose and living with very little power. The schemes convinced us that it w supposed to be that way, but our eyes of understanding are beginning to be flooded with light and we allowing God to root us and ground us in His kind of love. Our redemption was not meant for our spi only and Jesus has invited us into the process of discovering just how effective and expansive H redemption is. In fact, we each are truly a new creation and learning how to live as such. Old minds are being shed as we partner with the Holy Spirit in the renewing of our minds and transformation revealed. Our true identity, our godly purpose and the surpassing greatness of God's power all cha the game.

Yes, there are forces in our midst that resist us as we forge ahead so we must keep our eyes on where are headed and refuse to be distracted or dissuaded. We must receive the grace to persevere: living *fr* the Kingdom of God, drawing from our godly inheritance, and being led by our spirits. "On Earth as i in Heaven" is the goal set before us—and it will come to pass. Will you play an active role and be part the expansion? Will you partner with the Holy Spirit to be transformed so that, as the Kingdom of God active in your own life, the Kingdom of Heaven will be released all around you? The Kingdom of G **must come within you** so that the Kingdom of Heaven can come all around you—Christ in you, the ho of glory *for the world.*

What an adventure!

Summary

Ephesians At-a-Glance

- Live from your God-given identity and, by the way, I pray God expands it!
- Remember where He found you? Now remember how dramatically He has changed you. Get the vision for where He is taking you.
- Don't lose heart no matter the circumstances - submerge yourself in God and live from that reality. Keep the vision of where you are headed before your eyes.
- We are many yet one. Each has a personal destiny in God and is gifted and connected to the Body of Christ in a way that can bring that destiny forth. Just as important: we need each other to live well because we are connected and interlocking like a jigsaw puzzle. No missing pieces allowed. It's time to grow up and live from our newness.
- Who you truly are (the new you - in Christ and spirit led) should affect how you relate to others; be aware of that and live **from** the Kingdom of God toward the world around you.
- The armor of God depicts your true identity—it is who you are and it is who you are becoming: saved, righteous, in Truth, in Peace, flowing with faith and going forth with the Word of God making the way.

May the eyes of your understanding be increasingly flooded with LIGHT!

Appendix A

Exousia (G1849):

Mat 7:29; Mat 8:9; Mat 9:6; Mat 9:8; Mat 10:1; Mat 21:23; Mat 21:24; Mat 21:27; Mat 28:18; Mar 1:22; Mar 1:27; Mar 2:10; Mar 3:15; Mar 6:7; Mar 11:28; Mar 11:29; Mar 11:33; Mar 13:34; Luk 4:6; Luk 4:32; Luk 4:36; Luk 5:24; Luk 7:8; Luk 9:1; Luk 10:19; Luk 12:5; Luk 12:11; Luk 19:17; Luk 20:2; Luk 20:8; Luk 20:20; Luk 22:53; Luk 23:7; Joh 1:12; Joh 5:27; Joh 10:18; Joh 17:2; Joh 19:10; Joh 19:11; Act 1:7; Act 5:4; Act 8:19; Act 9:14; Act 26:10; Act 26:12; Act 26:18; Rom 9:21; Rom 13:1; Rom 13:2; Rom 13:3; 1Co 7:37; 1Co 8:9; 1Co 9:4; 1Co 9:5; 1Co 9:6; 1Co 9:12; 1Co 9:18; 1Co 11:10; 1Co 15:24; 2Co 10:8; 2Co 13:10; Eph 1:21; Eph 2:2; Eph 3:10; Eph 6:12; Col 1:13; Col 1:16; Col 2:10; Col 2:15; 2Th 3:9; Tit 3:1; Heb 13:10; 1Pe 3:22; Jud 1:25; Rev 2:26; Rev 6:8; Rev 9:3; Rev 9:10; Rev 9:19; Rev 11:6; Rev 12:10; Rev 13:2; Rev 13:4; Rev 13:5; Rev 13:7; Rev 13:12; Rev 14:18; Rev 16:9; Rev 17:12; Rev 17:13; Rev 18:1; Rev 20:6; Rev 22:14

Dunamis (G1411):

Mat 6:13; Mat 7:22; Mat 11:20; Mat 11:21; Mat 11:23; Mat 13:54; Mat 13:58; Mat 14:2; Mat 22:29; Mat 24:29; Mat 24:30; Mat 25:15; Mat 26:64; Mar 5:30; Mar 6:2; Mar 6:5; Mar 6:14; Mar 9:1; Mar 9:39; Mar 12:24; Mar 13:25; Mar 13:26; Mar 14:62; Luk 1:17; Luk 1:35; Luk 4:14; Luk 4:36; Luk 5:17; Luk 6:19; Luk 8:46; Luk 9:1; Luk 10:13; Luk 10:19; Luk 19:37; Luk 21:26; Luk 21:27; Luk 22:69; Luk 24:49; Act 1:8; Act 2:22; Act 3:12; Act 4:7; Act 4:33; Act 6:8; Act 8:10; Act 8:13; Act 10:38; Act 19:11; Rom 1:4; Rom 1:16; Rom 1:20; Rom 8:38; Rom 9:17; Rom 15:13; Rom 15:19; 1Co 1:18; 1Co 1:24; 1Co 2:4; 1Co 2:5; 1Co 4:19; 1Co 4:20; 1Co 5:4; 1Co 6:14; 1Co 12:10; 1Co 12:28; 1Co 12:29; 1Co 14:11; 1Co 15:24; 1Co 15:43; 1Co 15:56; 2Co 1:8; 2Co 4:7; 2Co 6:7; 2Co 8:3; 2Co 12:9; 2Co 12:12; 2Co 13:4; Gal 3:5; Eph 1:19; Eph 1:21; Eph 3:7; Eph 3:16; Eph 3:20; Php 3:10; Col 1:11; Col 1:29; 1Th 1:5; 2Th 1:7; 2Th 1:11; 2Th 2:9; 2Ti 1:7; 2Ti 1:8; 2Ti 3:5; Heb 1:3; Heb 2:4; Heb 6:5; Heb 7:16; Heb 11:11; Heb 11:34; 1Pe 1:5; 1Pe 3:22; 2Pe 1:3; 2Pe 1:16; 2Pe 2:11; Rev 1:16; Rev 3:8; Rev 4:11; Rev 5:12; Rev 7:12; Rev 11:17; Rev 12:10; Rev 13:2; Rev 15:8; Rev 17:13; Rev 18:3; Rev 19:1

Energia (G1753):

Eph 1:19; Eph 3:7; Eph 4:16; Php 3:21; Col 1:29; Col 2:12; 2Th 2:9; 2Th 2:11

Kratos (G2904):

Luk 1:51; Act 19:20; Eph 1:19; Eph 6:10; Col 1:11; 1Ti 6:16; Heb 2:14; 1Pe 4:11; 1Pe 5:11; Jud 1:25; Rev 1:6; Rev 5:13

Ischus (G2479):

Mar 12:30; Mar 12:33; Luk 10:27; Eph 1:19; Eph 6:10; 2Th 1:9; 1Pe 4:11; 2Pe 2:11; Rev 5:12; Rev 7:12; Rev 18:2

Appendix B*

1Ki 3:11-12 God said to him (Solomon), "Because you have asked this thing and have not asked for yourself long life, nor have asked riches for yourself, nor have you asked for the life of your enemies, but have asked for yourself discernment to **understand** justice, behold, I have done according to your words. Behold, I have given you a wise and **understanding** heart…(NASB)

Psa 28:5 Because they did not **understand** the works of the LORD nor the deeds of His hands, He will tear them down and not build them up.

Psa 32:9 Do not be as the horse or as the mule which has no **understanding**, whose trappings include bit and bridle to hold them in check, otherwise they will not come near to you.

Psa 49:20 Man in his pomp, yet without **understanding**, is like the beasts that perish.

Psa 119:27 Make me **understand** the way of Your precepts, so I will meditate on Your wonders.

Psa 119:34 Give me **understanding** that I may observe Your law and keep it with all my heart.

Psa 119:73 Your hands made me and fashioned me. Give me **understanding** that I may learn Your commandments.

Psa 119:104 From Your precepts I get **understanding**. Therefore, I hate every false way.

Psa 119:125 I am Your servant. Give me **understanding** that I may know Your testimonies.

Psa 119:144 Your testimonies are righteous forever. Give me **understanding** that I may live.

Psa 119:169 Let my cry come before You, O Lord. Give me **understanding** according to Your word.

Pro 10:13 On the lips of the **understanding** wisdom is found, but a rod is for the back of him who lacks discernment.

Pro 14:8 The wisdom of the sensible is to **understand** his way, but the foolishness of fools is deceit.

---

* The word understanding has been used and bolded where the Hebrew word *bene* (H995) is used in the interlinear text.

Made in the USA
Middletown, DE
27 August 2018